© Copyright 2021 - All rights reserved.

You may not reproduce, duplicate or send the contents of this book without direct written permission from the author. You cannot hereby despite any circumstance blame the publisher or hold him or her to legal responsibility for any reparation, compensations, or monetary forfeiture owing to the information included herein, either in a direct or an indirect way.

Legal Notice: This book has copyright protection. You can use the book for personal purpose. You should not sell, use, alter, distribute, quote, take excerpts or paraphrase in part or whole the material contained in this book without obtaining the permission of the author first.

Disclaimer Notice: You must take note that the information in this document is for casual reading and entertainment purposes only. We have made every attempt to provide accurate, up to date and reliable information. We do not express or imply guarantees of any kind. The persons who read admit that the writer is not occupied in giving legal, financial, medical or other advice. We put this book content by sourcing various places.

Please consult a licensed professional before you try any techniques shown in this book. By going through this document, the book lover comes to an agreement that under no situation is the author accountable for any forfeiture, direct or indirect, which they may incur because of the use of material contained in this document, including, but not limited to, —errors, omissions, or inaccuracies.

THIS BOOK BELONGS TO

_____

Alphabet	Words
a	as in ant, aeroplane, apple, arrow, axe, etc.
b	as in bird, ball, basket, bulb, bat, butterfly, bun, etc.
c	as in camel, candle, cat, car, cap, cake, carrot, etc.
d	as in dates, duck, door, drum, dog, etc.
e	as in elephant, egg, envelope, ellipse, engine, etc.
f	as in fish, frog, flower, flag, finger, etc.
g	as in grapes, goat, gate, gun, guava, etc.
h	as in horse, hammer, house, hut, hat, hand, etc.
i	as in ink, insects, igloo, inch, etc.
j	as in jug, jar, jeep, jacket, etc.
k	as in key, kettle, king, kite, etc.
l	as in lion, leaf, lamp, lemon, lady finger, ladder, etc.
m	as in mango, mug, mat, mouse, moon, etc.
n	as in night, net, nest, nail, napkin, nose, etc.
o	as in olive, orange, ostrich, octopus, etc.
p	as in pen, pear, pigeon, pencil, peg, peacock etc.
q	as in quill, quilt, queue, quarter, etc.
r	as in rain, rose, rabbit, rug, etc.
s	as in sun, sofa, snake, soap, slipper, etc.
t	as in tree, tomato, tent, telephone, table, etc.
u	as in uncle, umbrella, under, unhappy, etc.
v	as in vegetable, vase, van, violin, etc.
w	as in wheat, watch, wall, window, etc.
x	as in box, ox, fox, wax, x-ray, etc.
y	as in yacht, yo-yo, yak, yellow etc.
z	as in zip, zebra, zig zag, zoo, etc.

color the Box

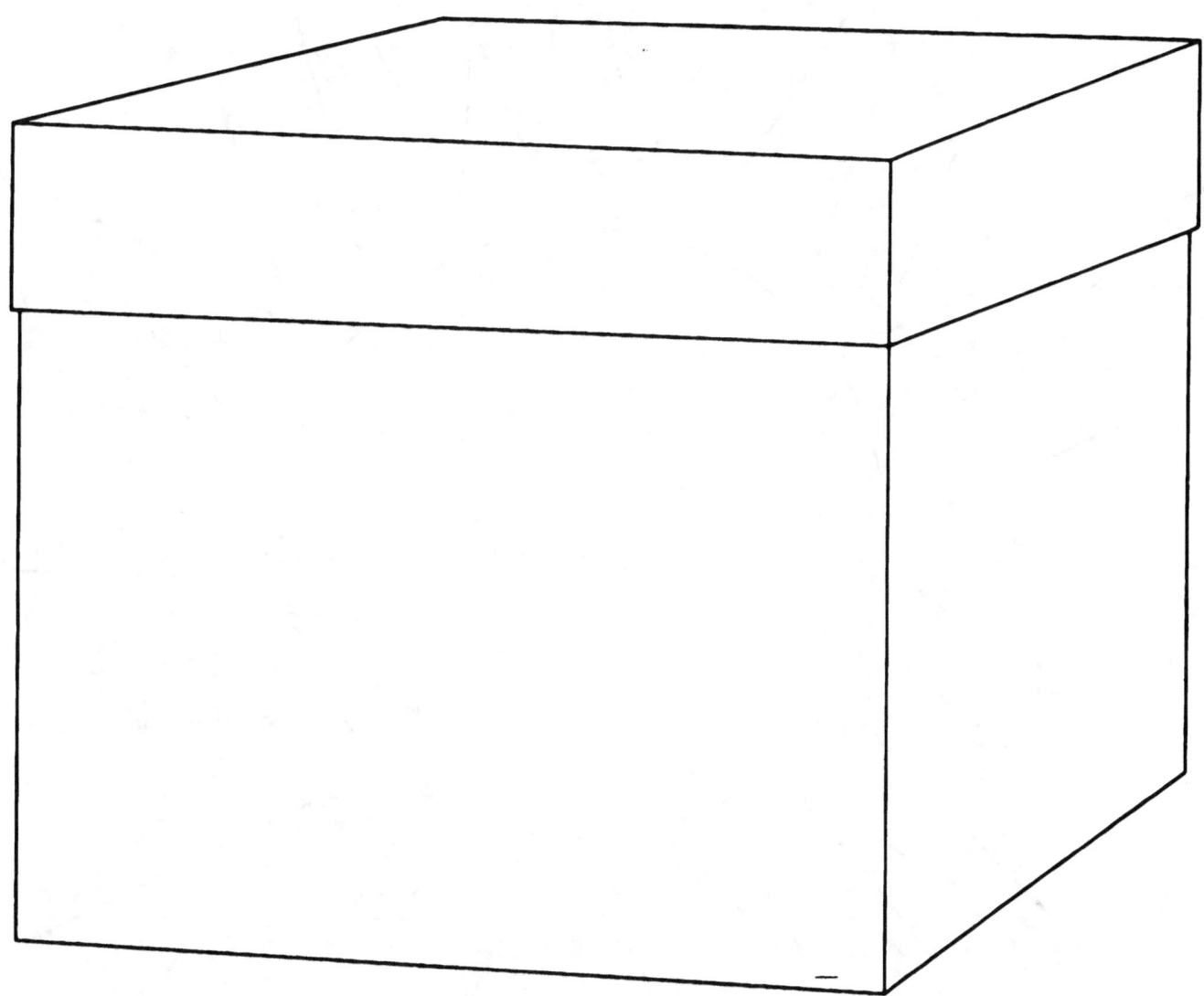

color the sun

color the mug

color the tomato

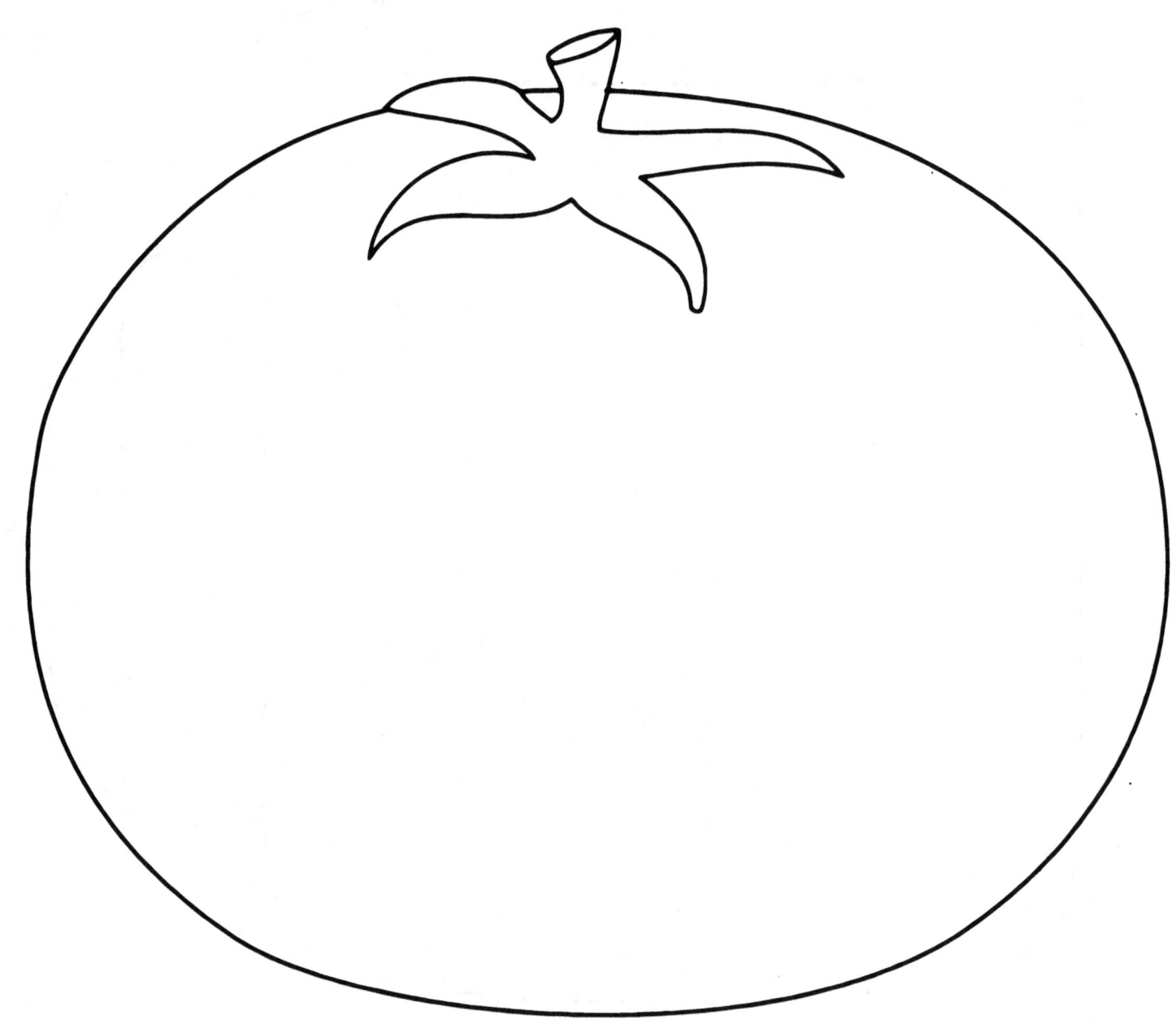

color the umbrella

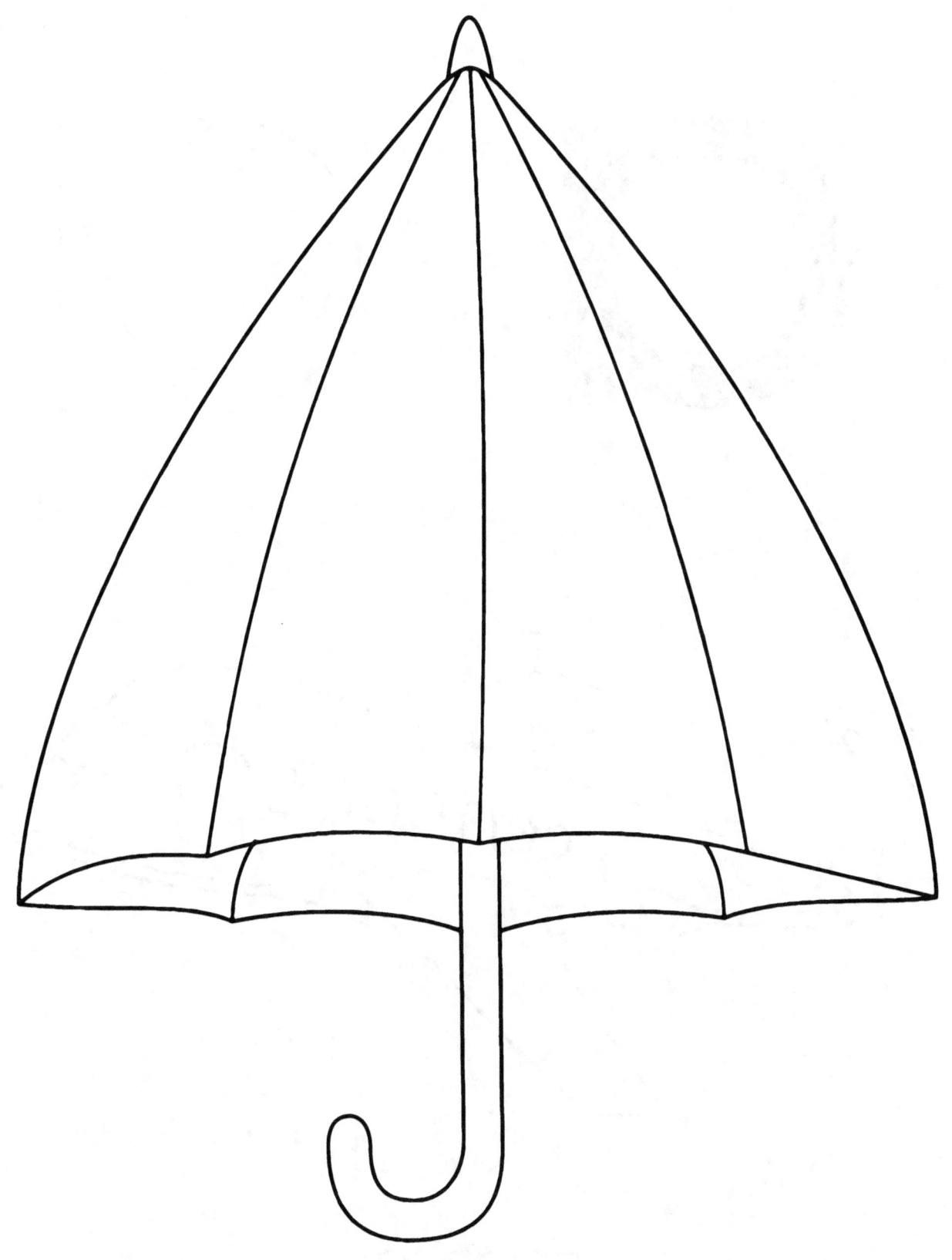

trace and color

 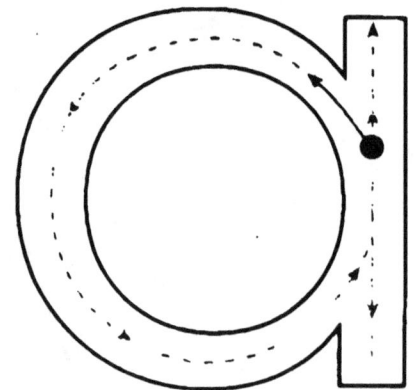

aeroplane

trace and color

apple   ant

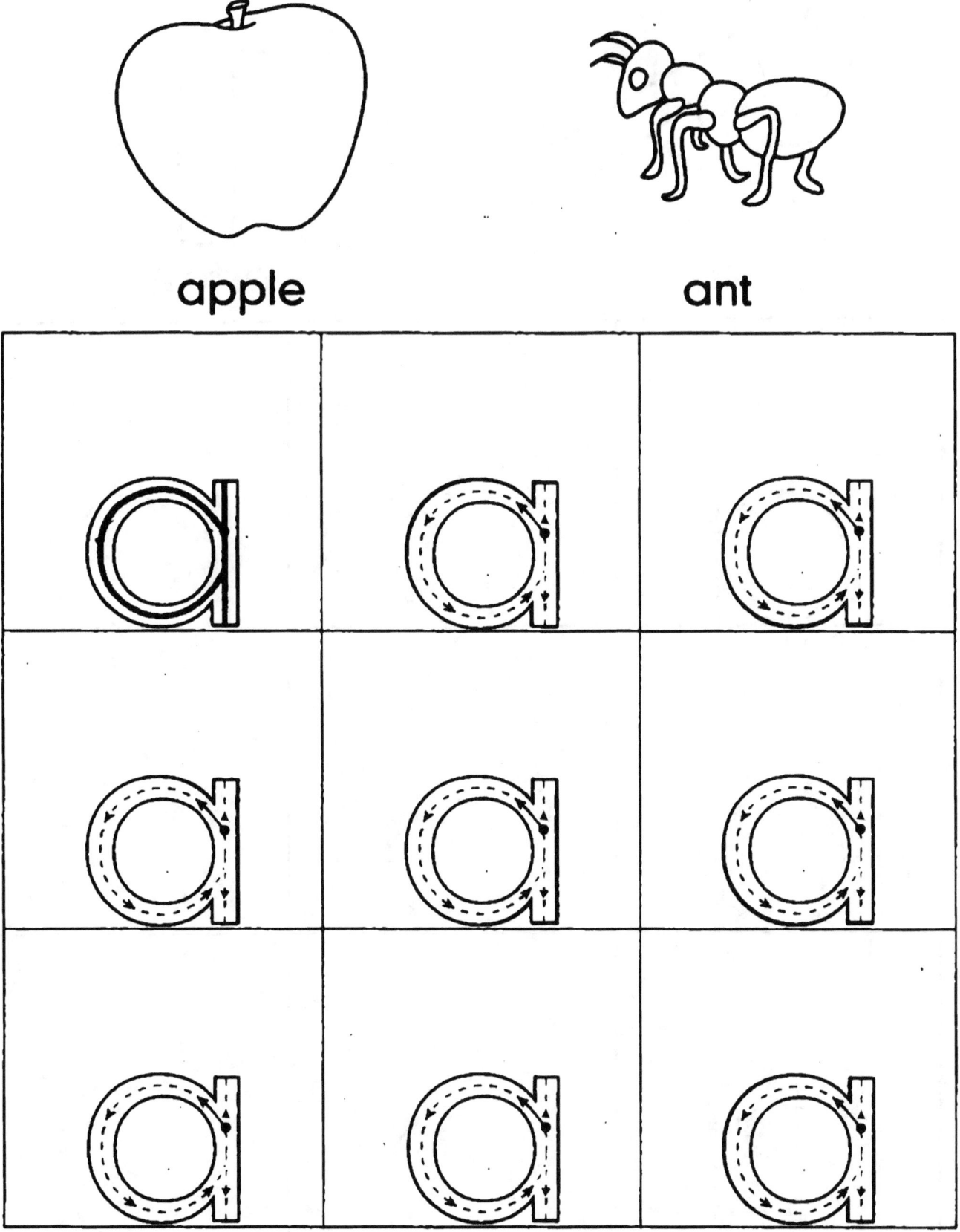

trace and color

axe

arrow

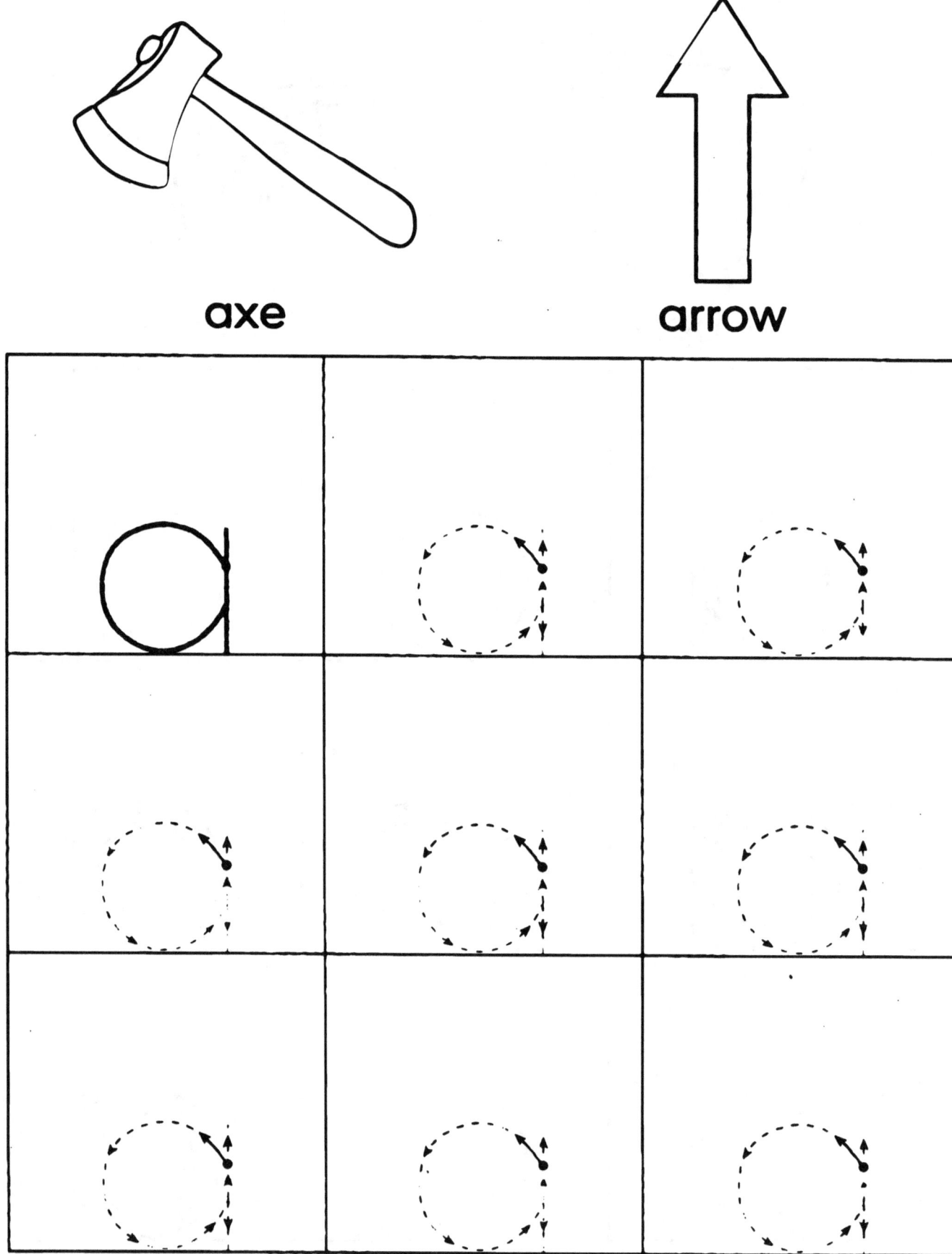

write and color

apricot

ambulance

a	a	a	a

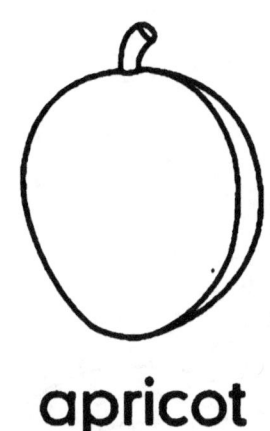

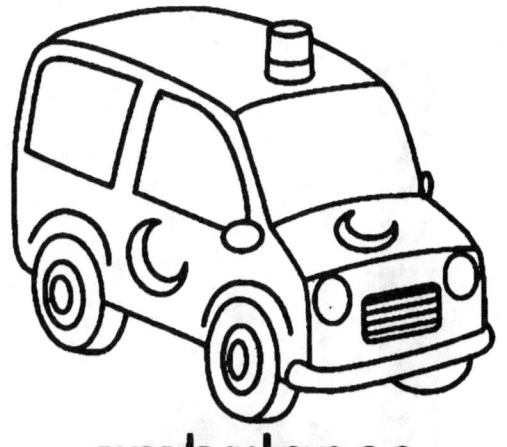

trace and color

bus

trace and color

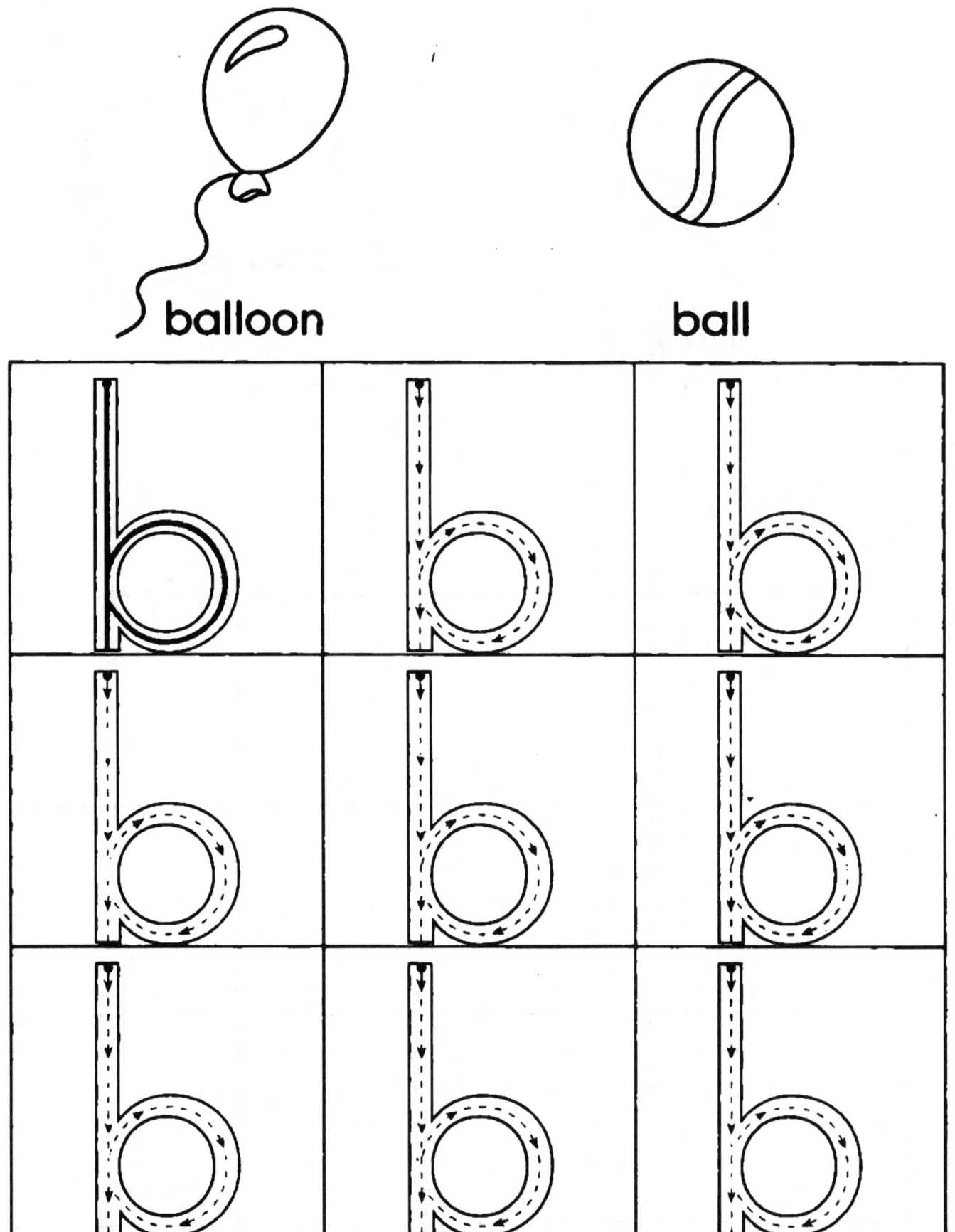

balloon   ball

write and color

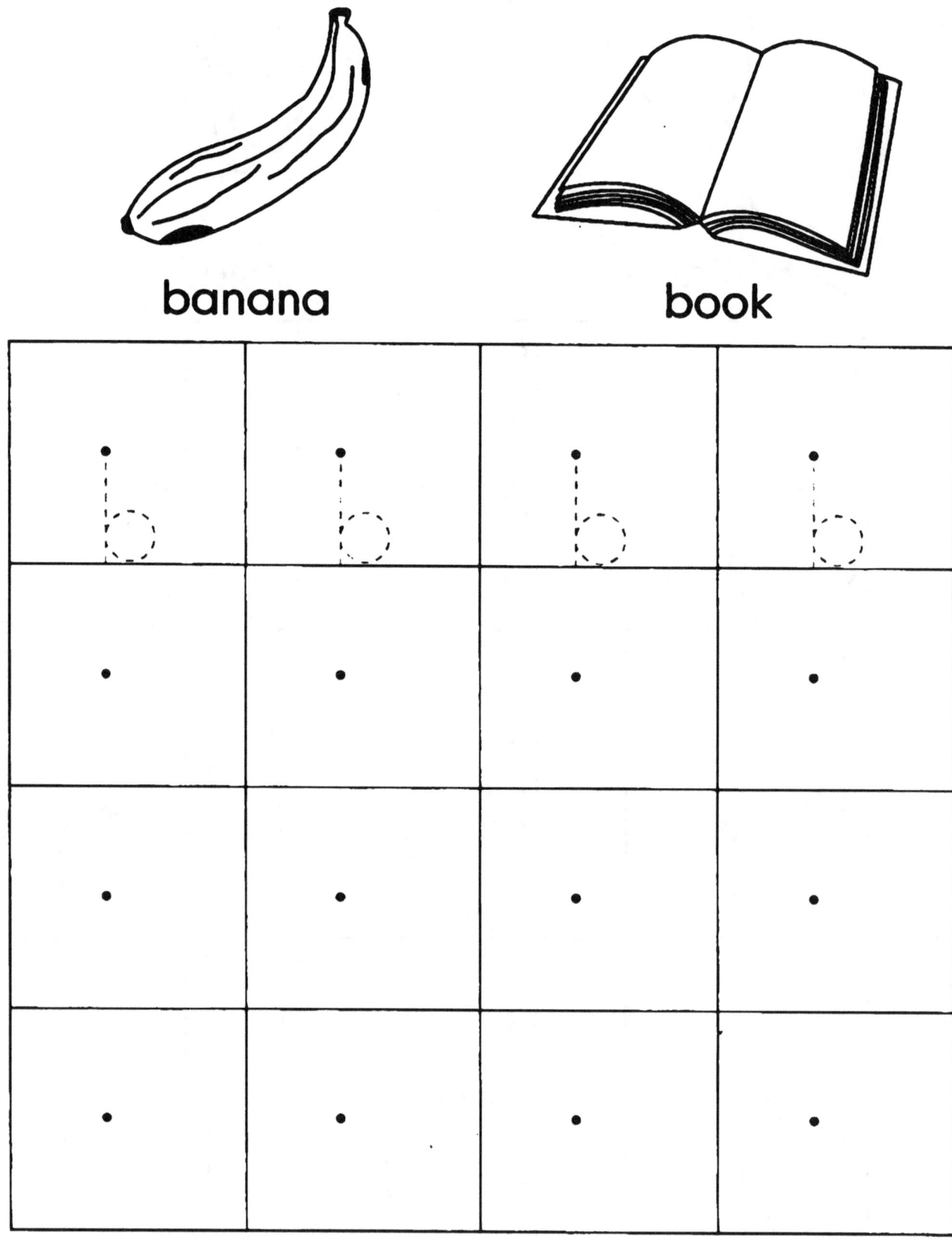

banana   book

trace and color

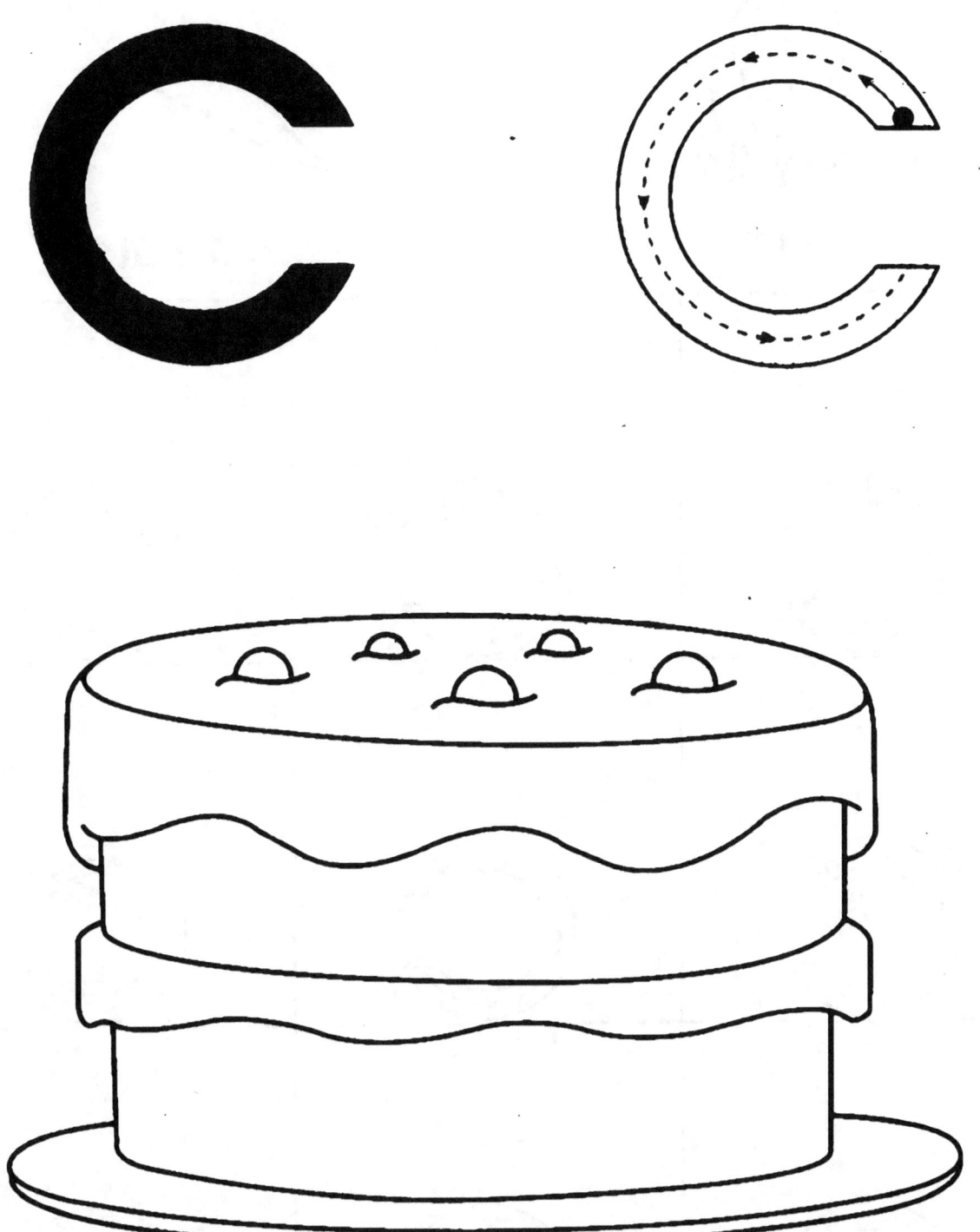

cake

trace and color

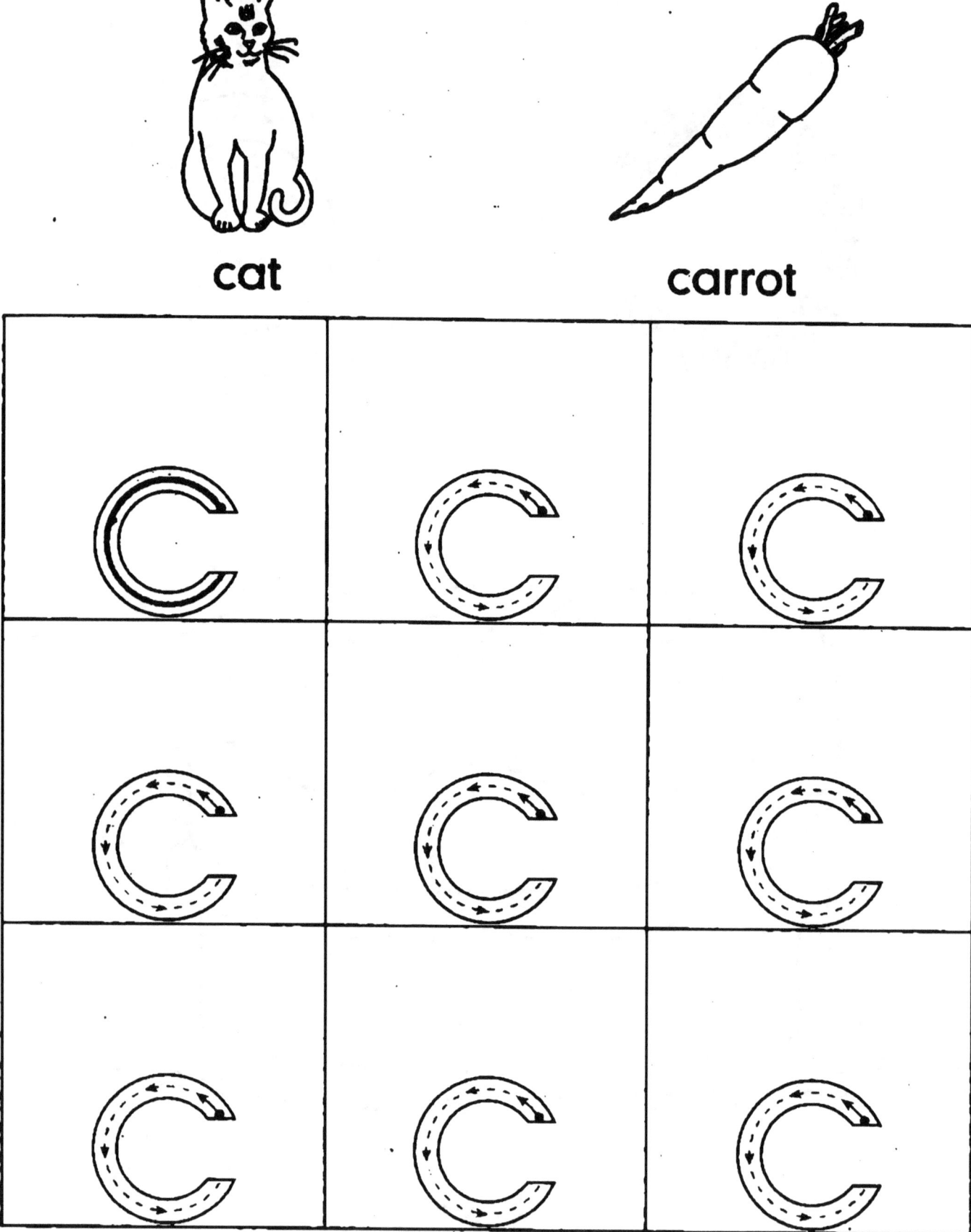

cat carrot

trace and color

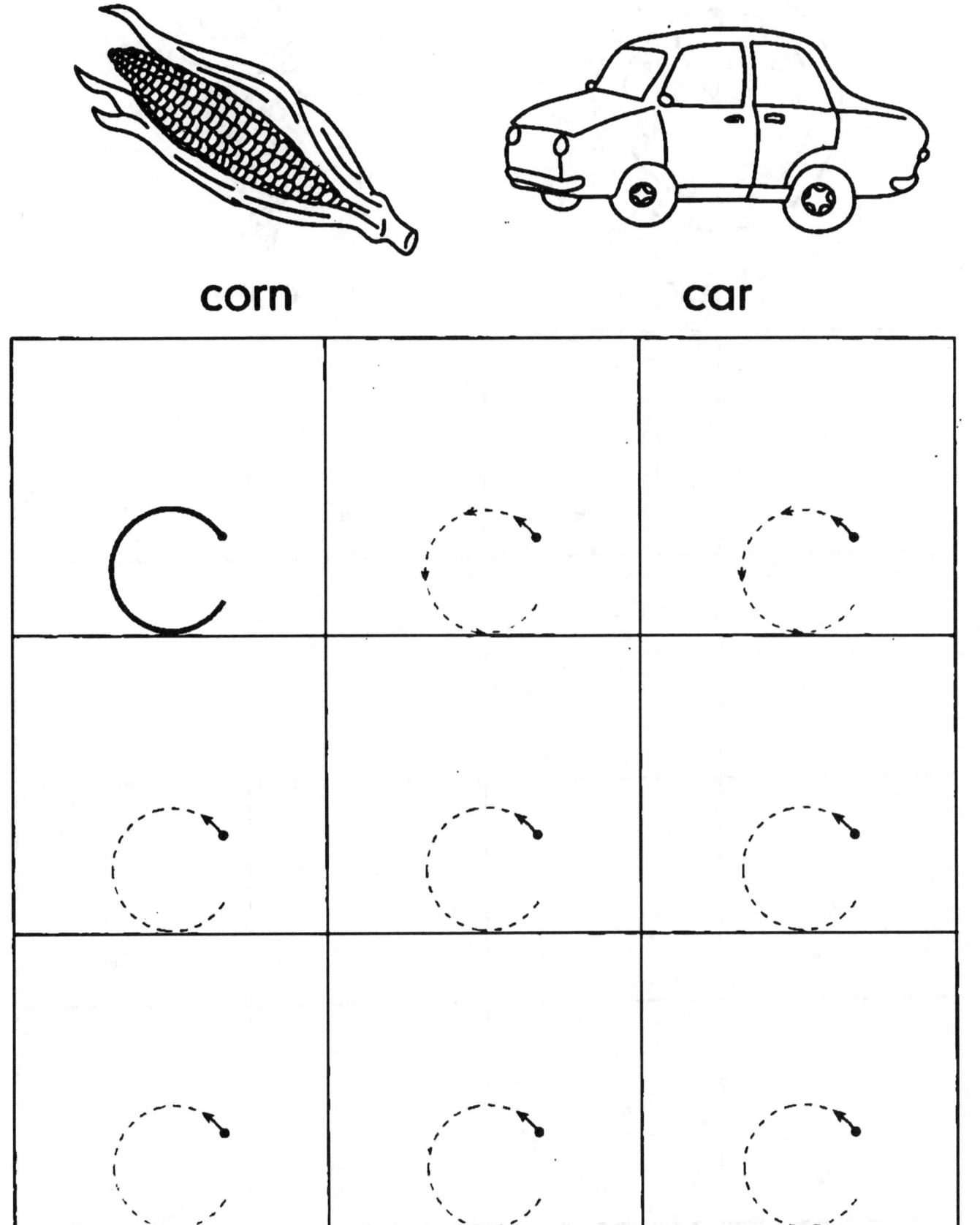

corn　　　　　car

write and color

clock

cone

trace and color

duck

trace and color

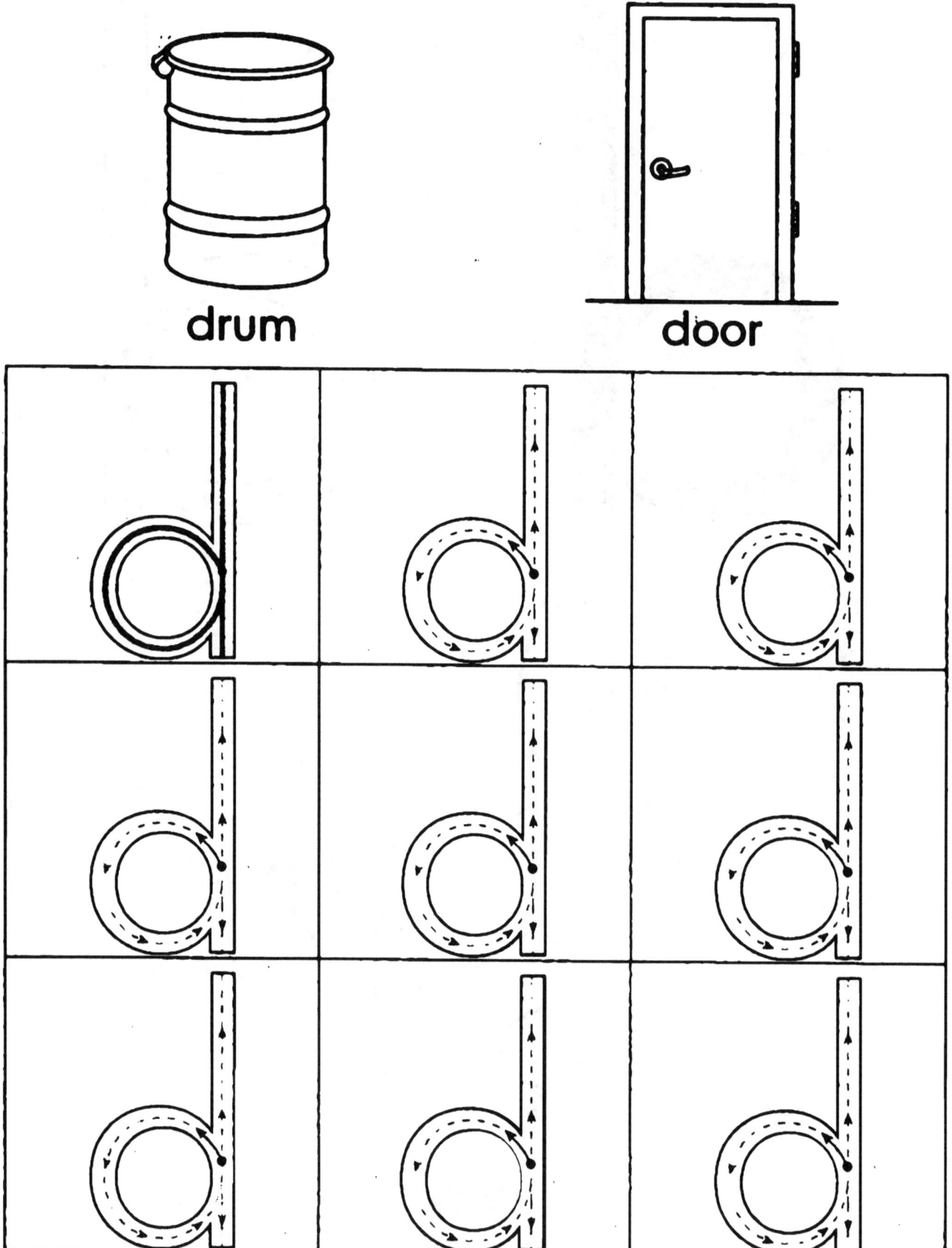

drum

door

write and color

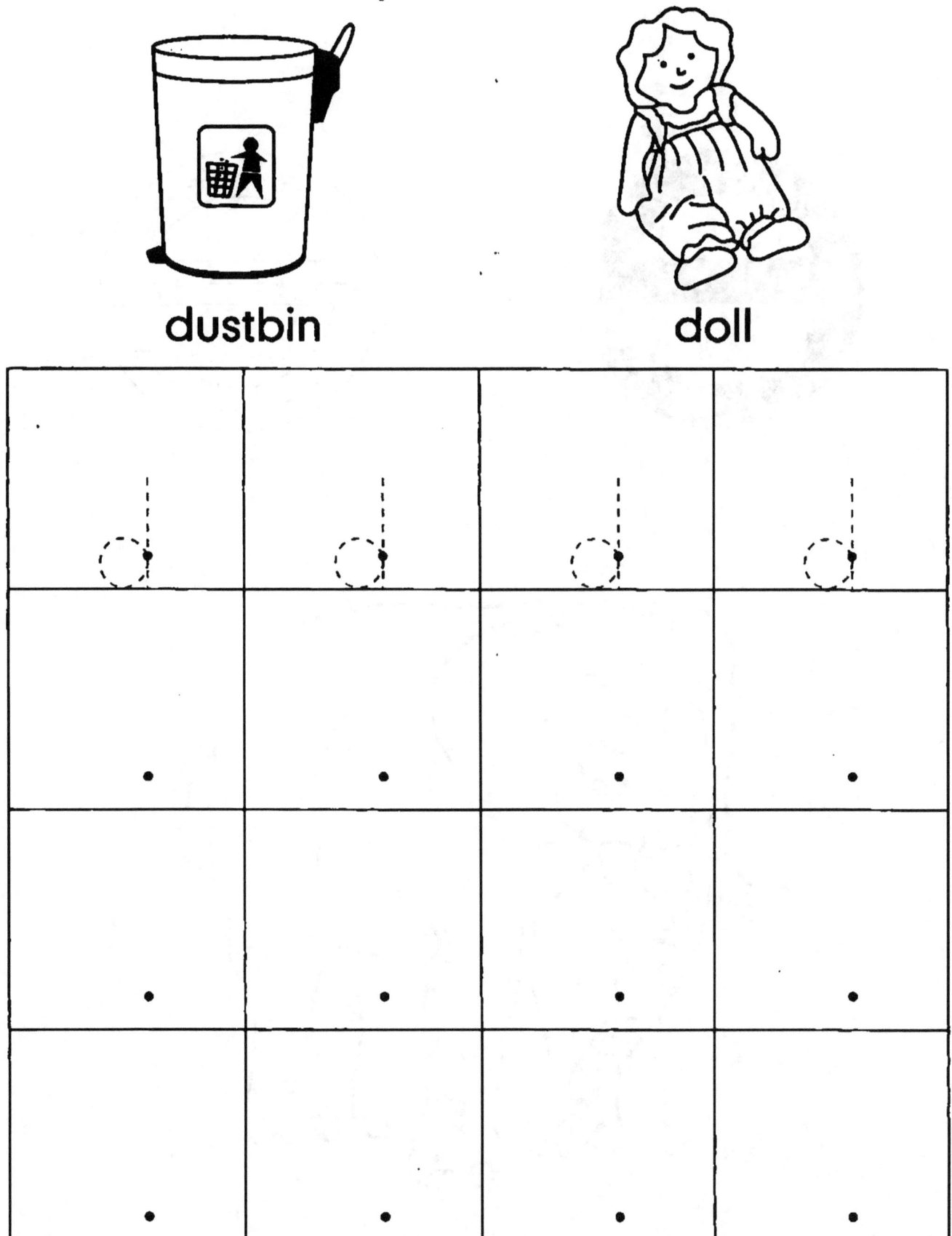

dustbin   doll

trace and color

elephant

trace and color

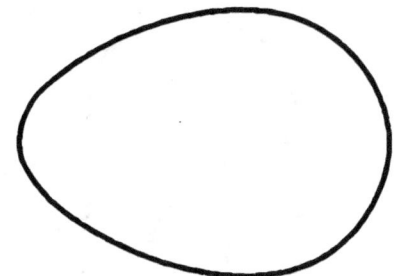 

egg   **envelope**

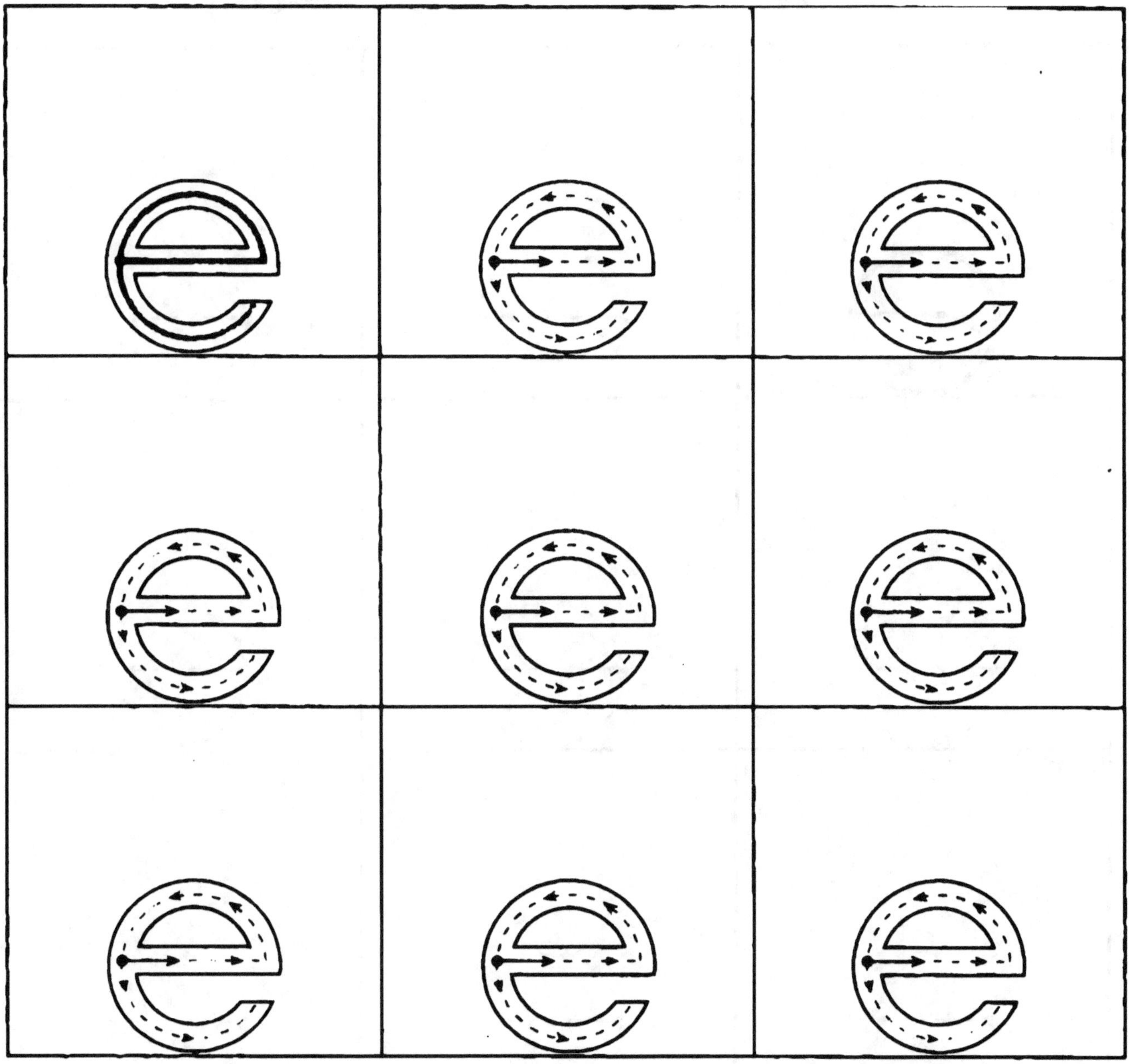

trace and color

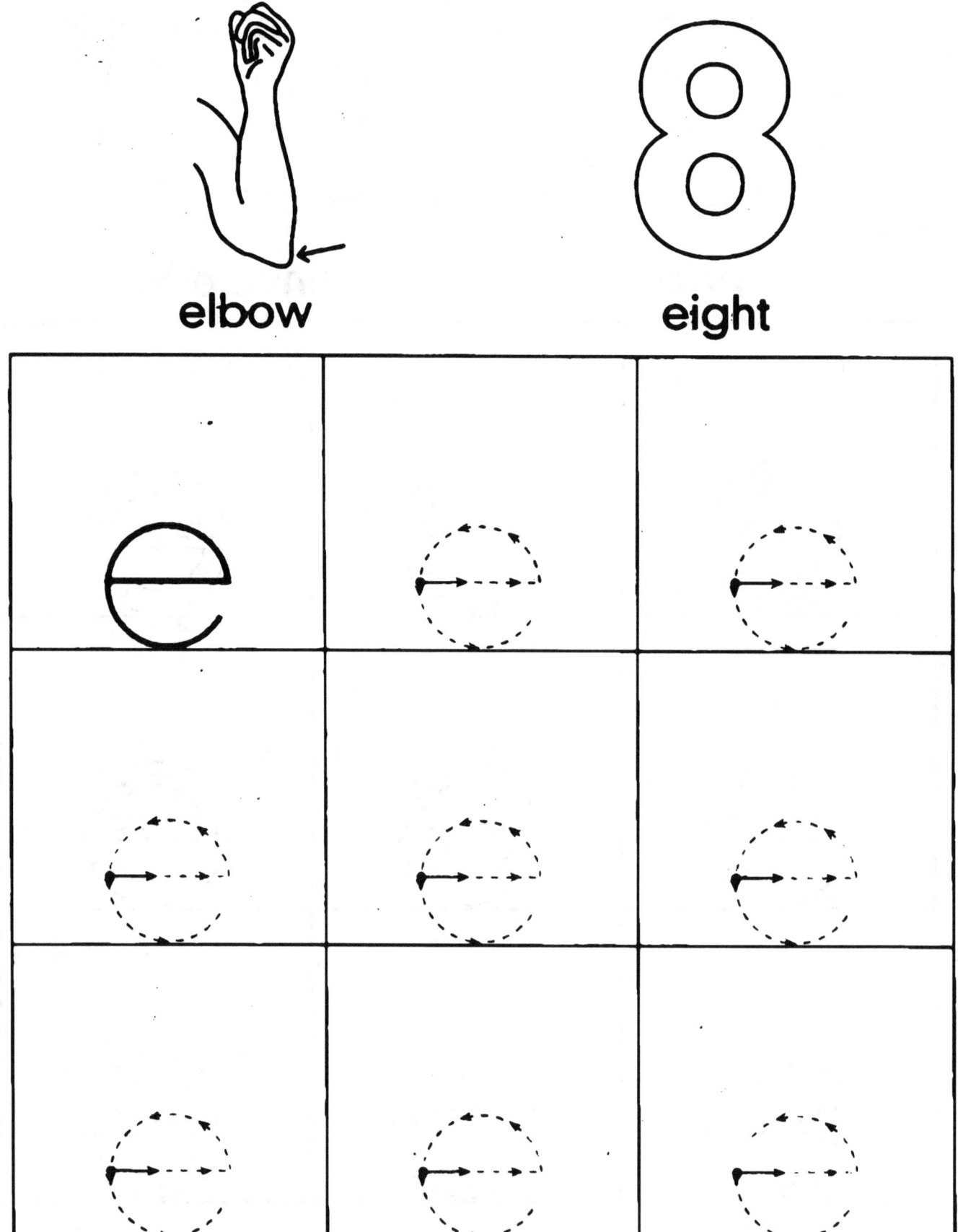

elbow   eight

write and color

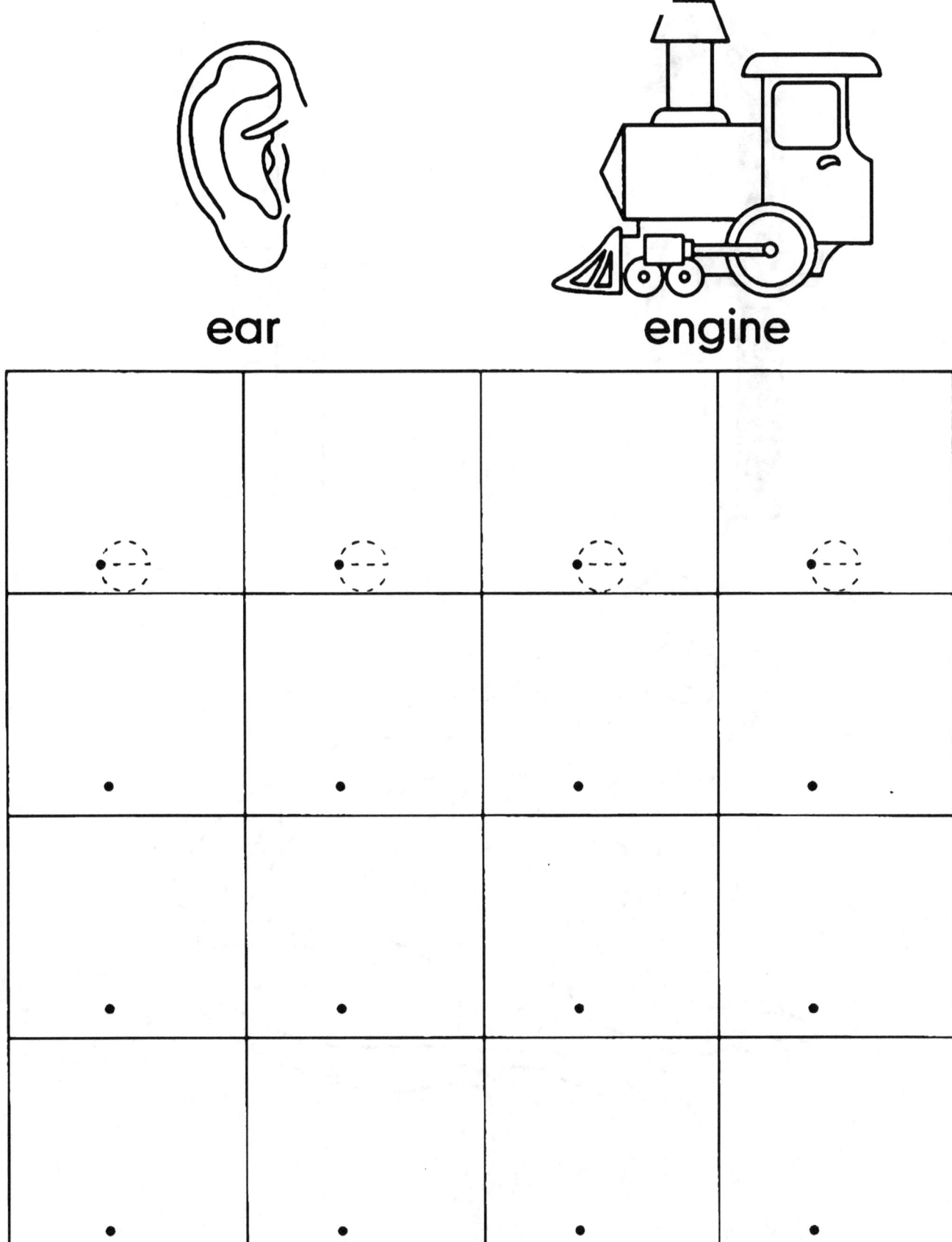

ear

engine

trace and color

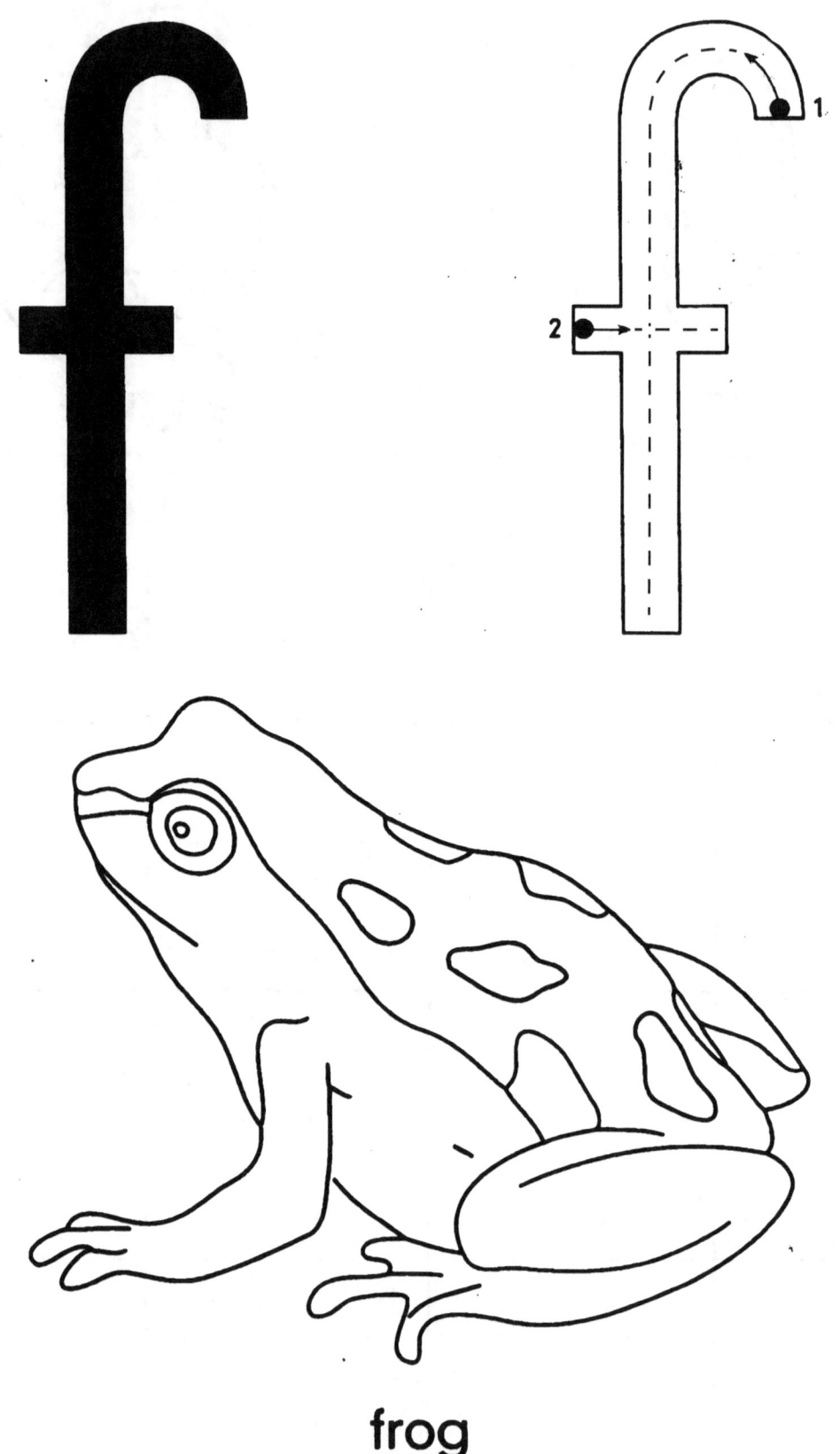

frog

trace and color

flower

finger

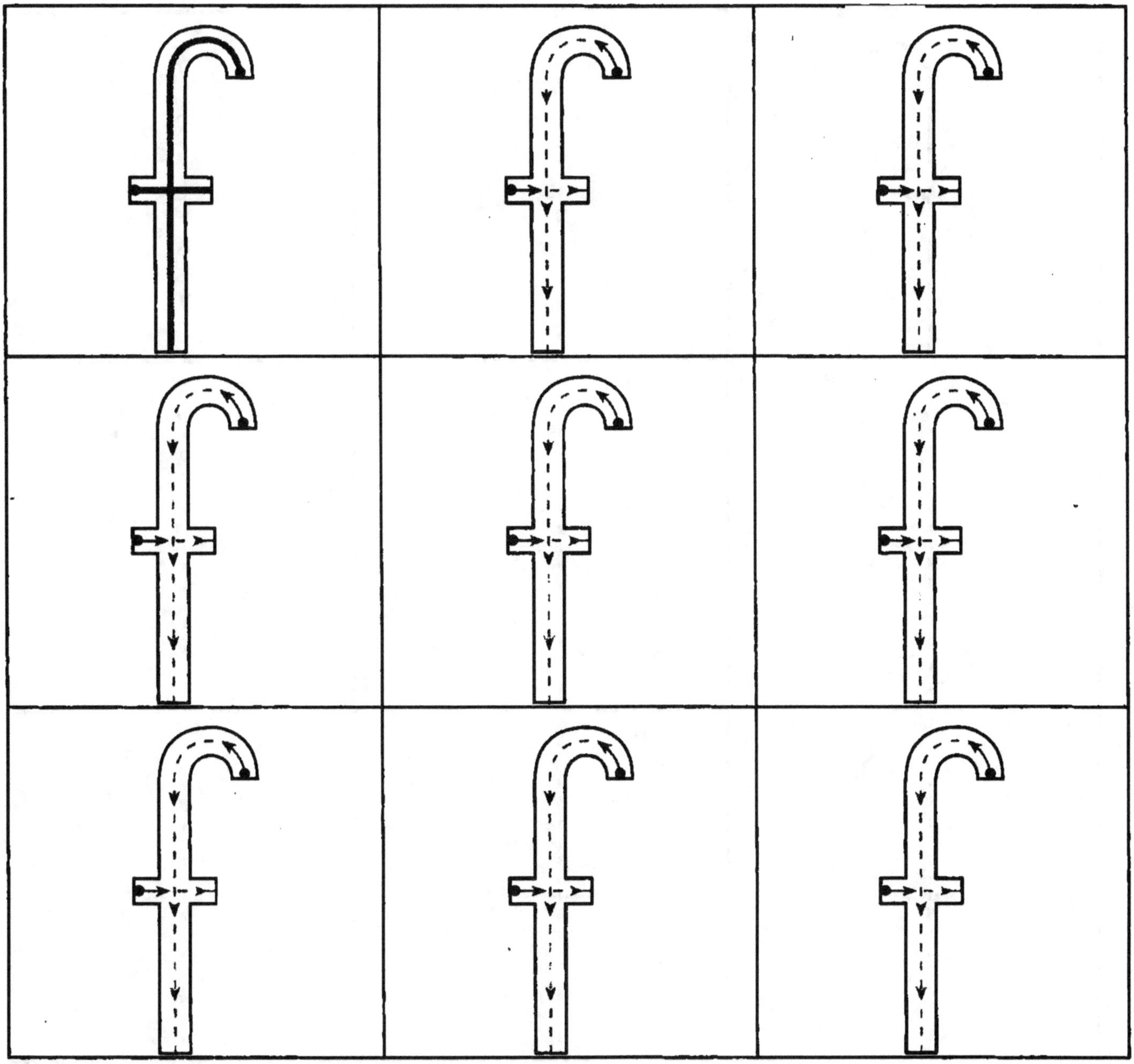

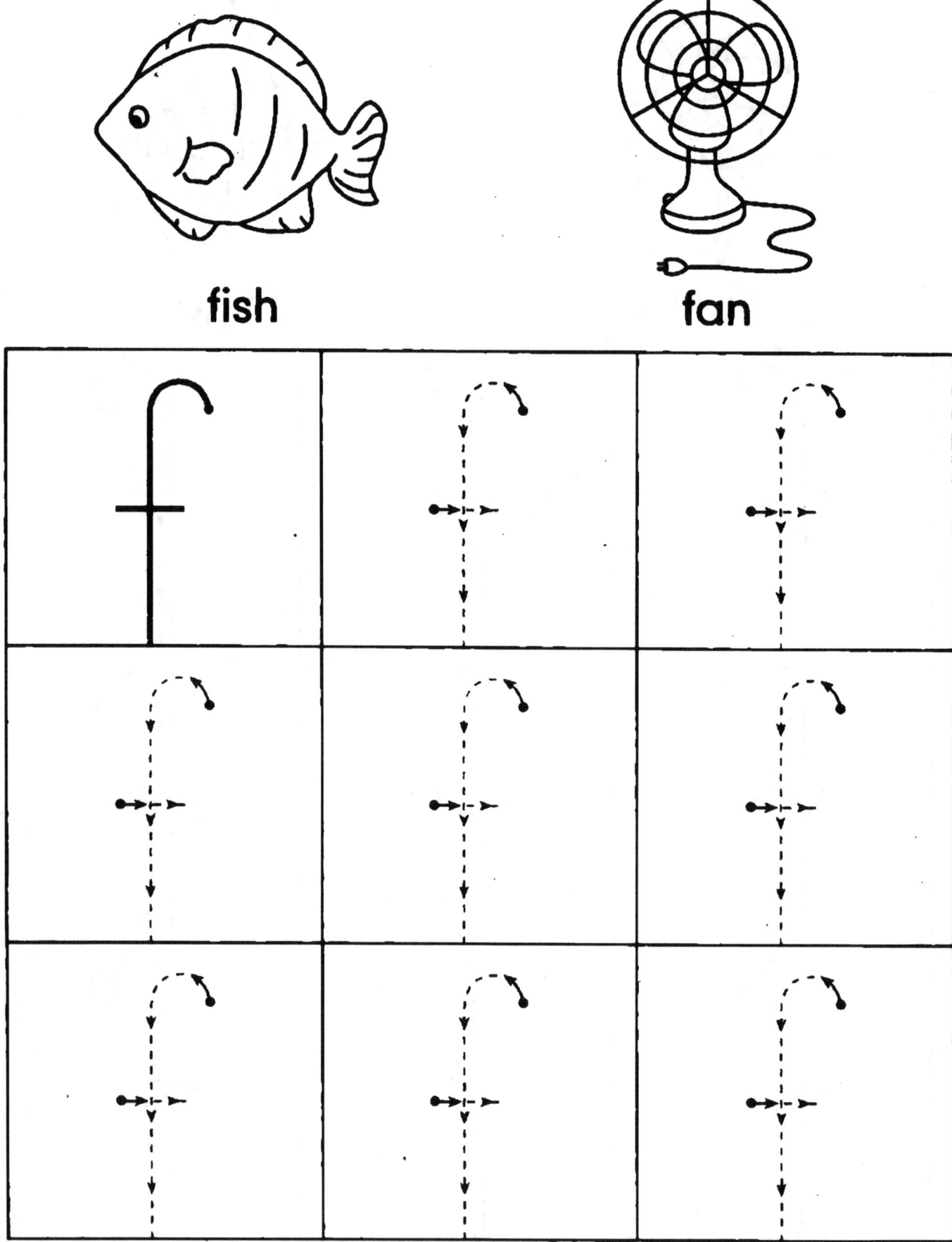

write and color

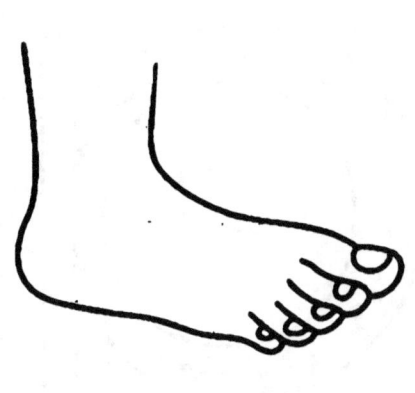
foot

fire

f	f	f	f
.	.	.	.
.	.	.	.
.	.	.	.

write and color

trace and color

grapes

trace and color

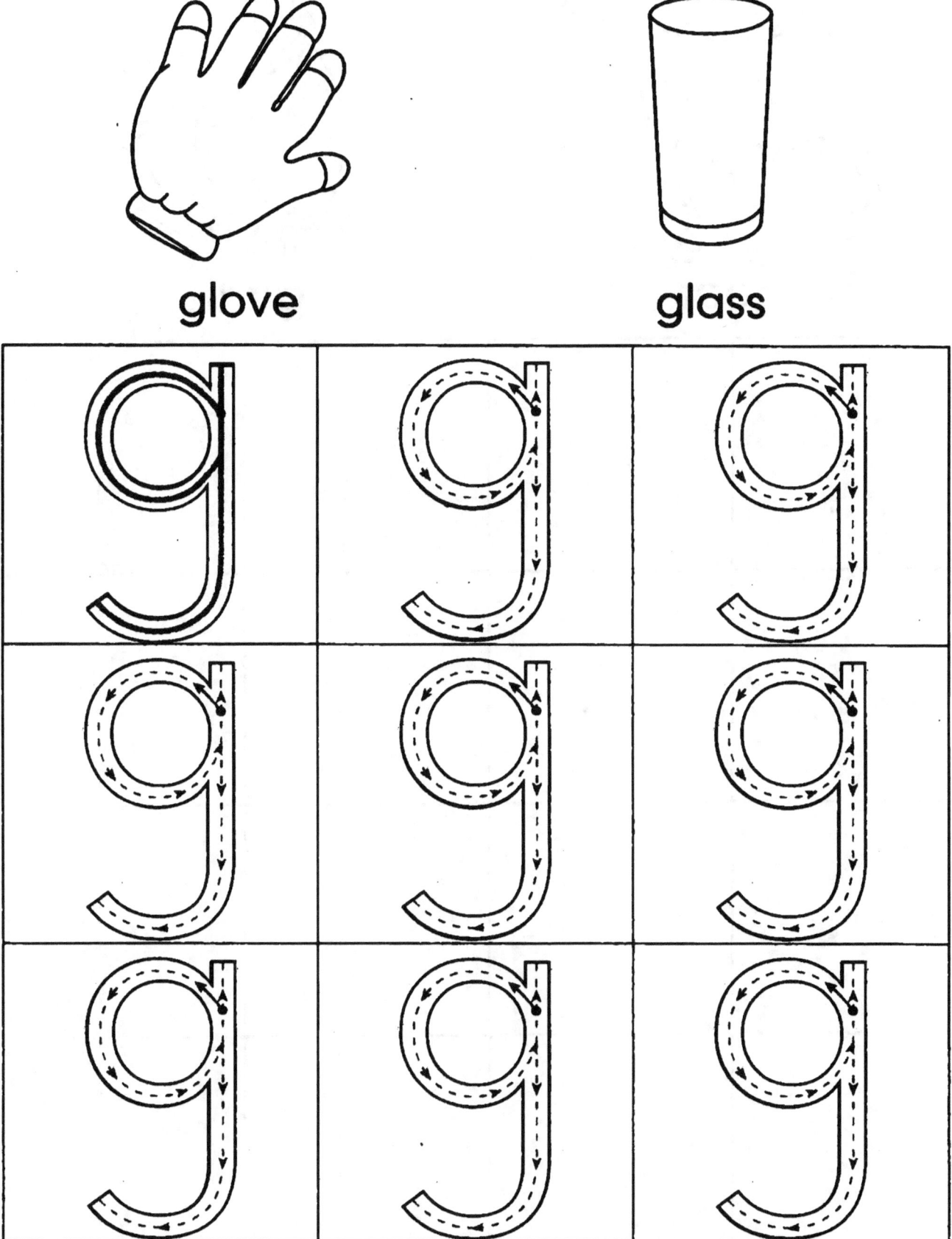

write and color

goat

garlic

9	9	9	9
.	.	.	.
.	.	.	.
.	.	.	.

trace and color

house

trace and color

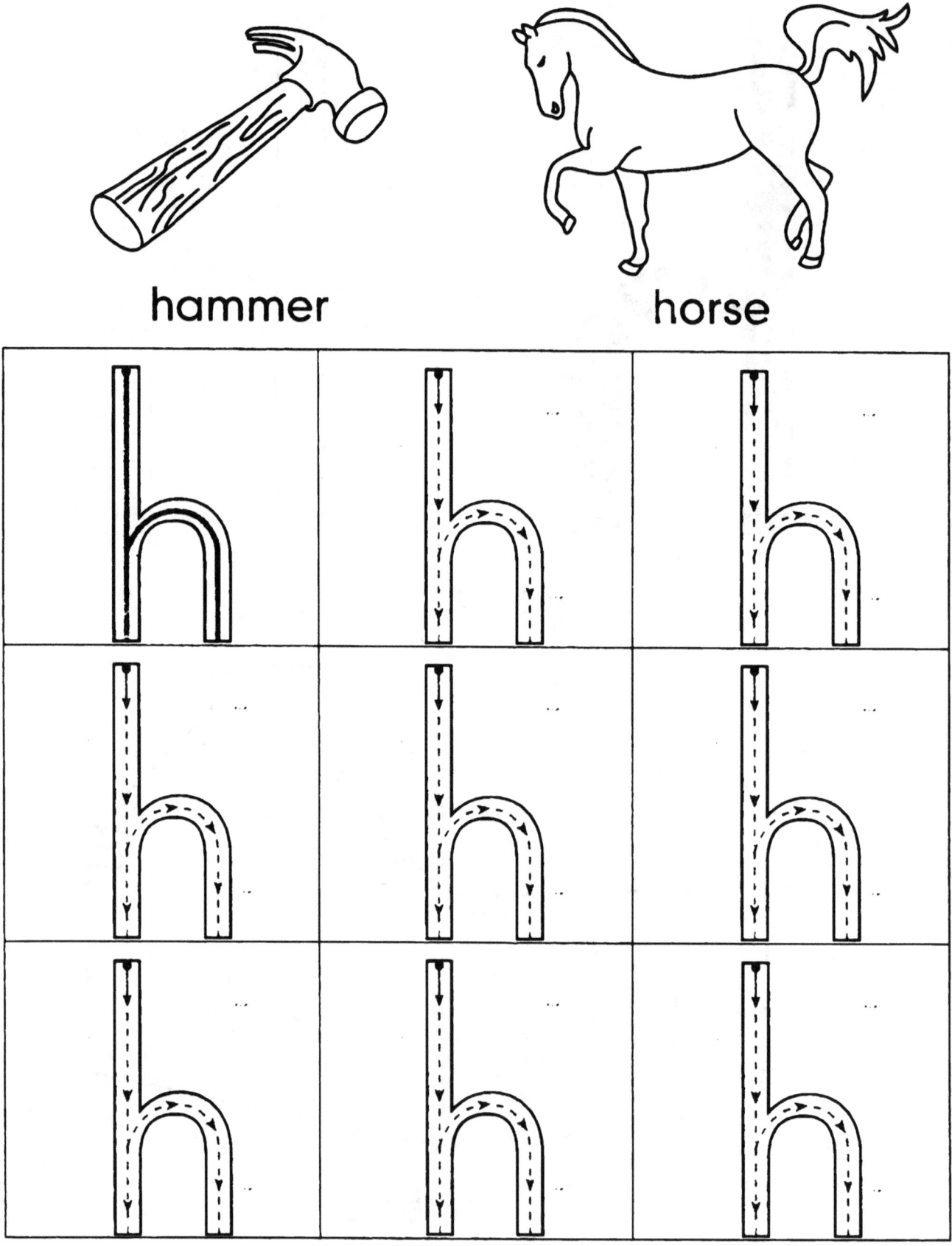

hammer · horse

trace and color

hen

helicopter

h	h	h	h

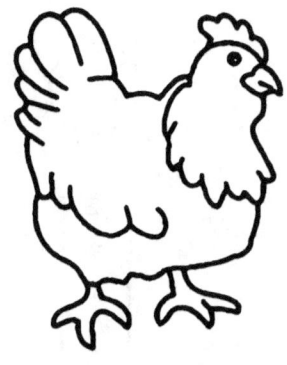

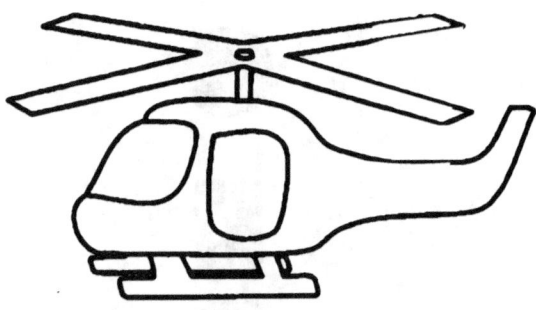

trace and color

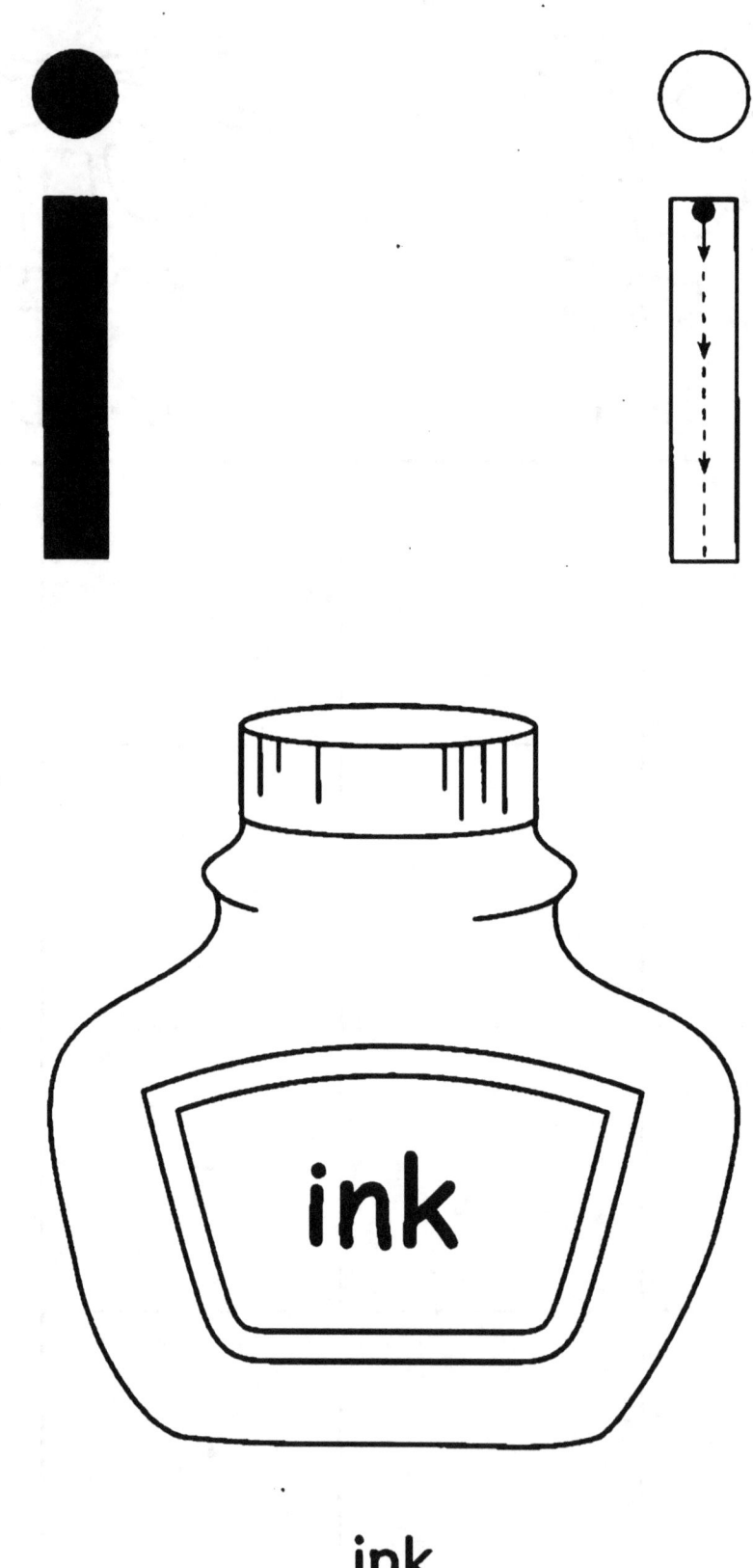

ink

write and color

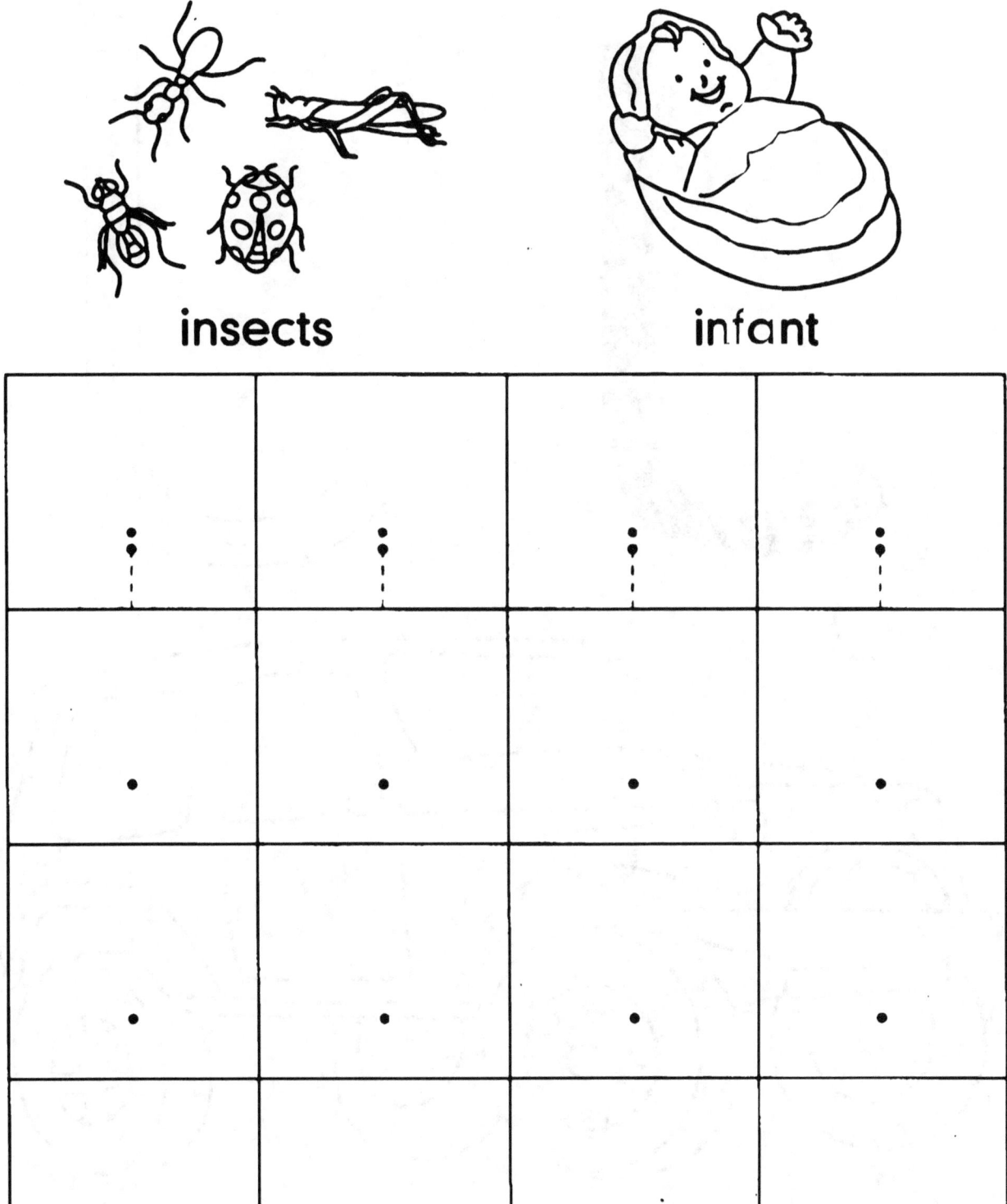

insects   infant

trace and color

jeep

trace and color

jelly   jam

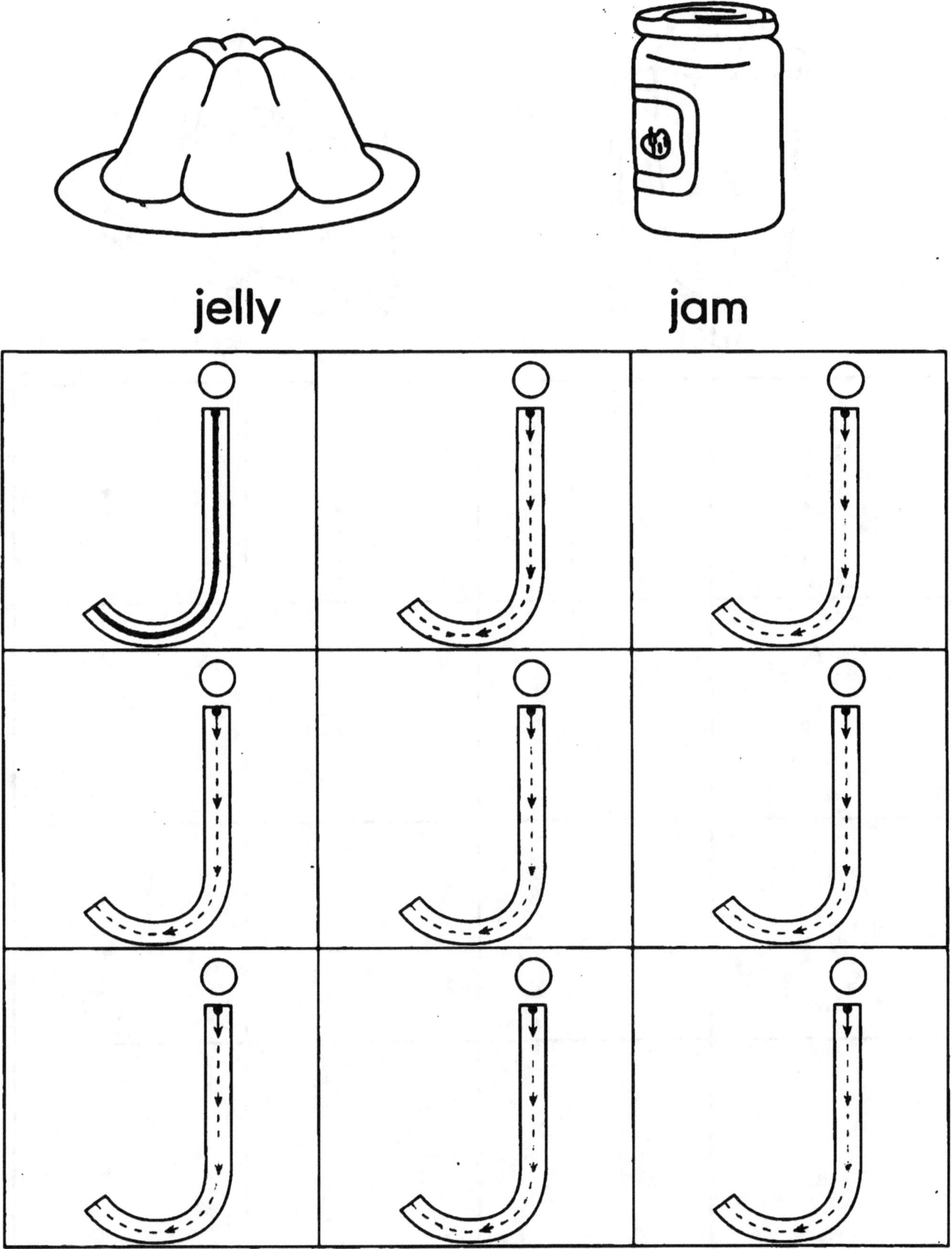

write and color

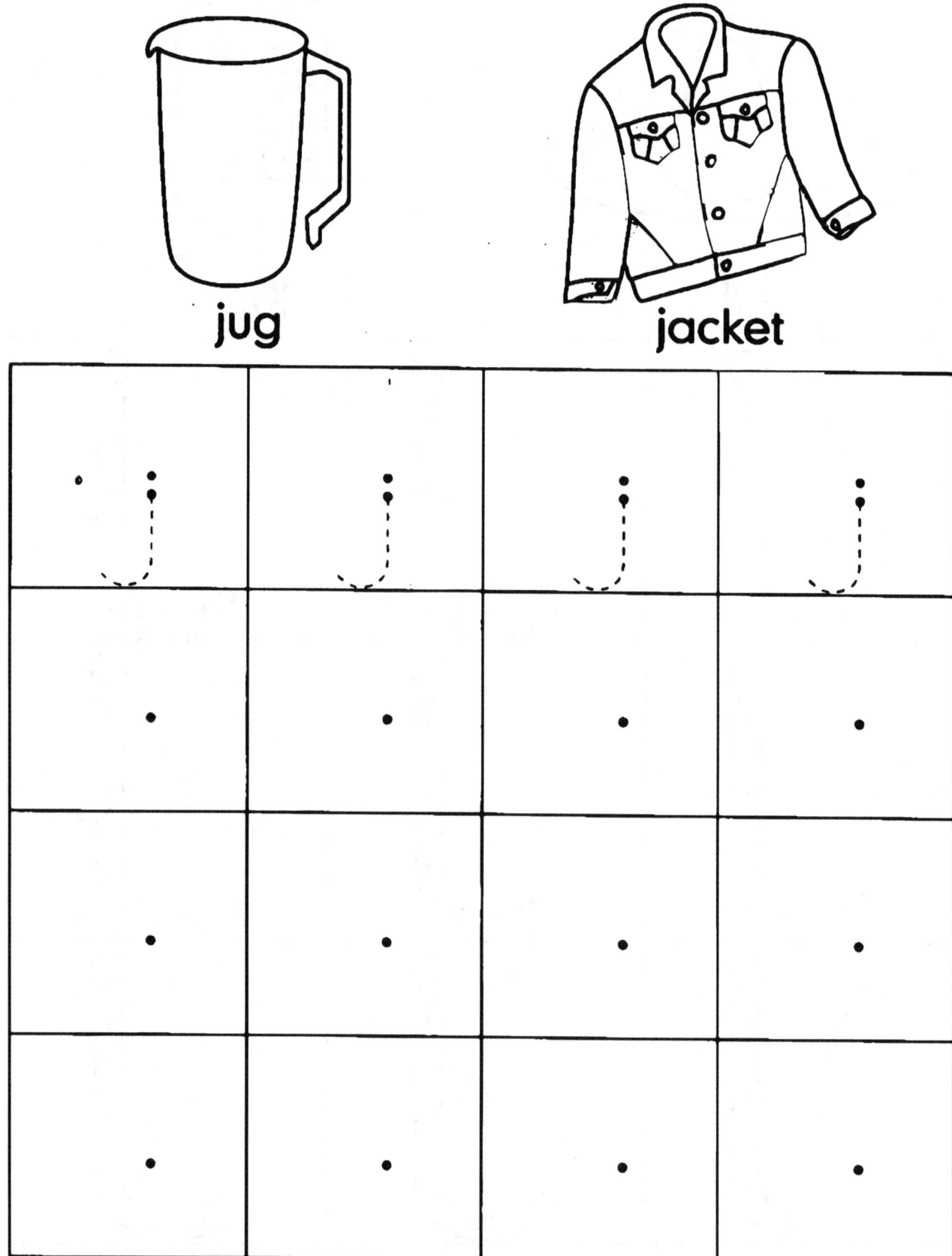

jug   jacket

trace and color

k k

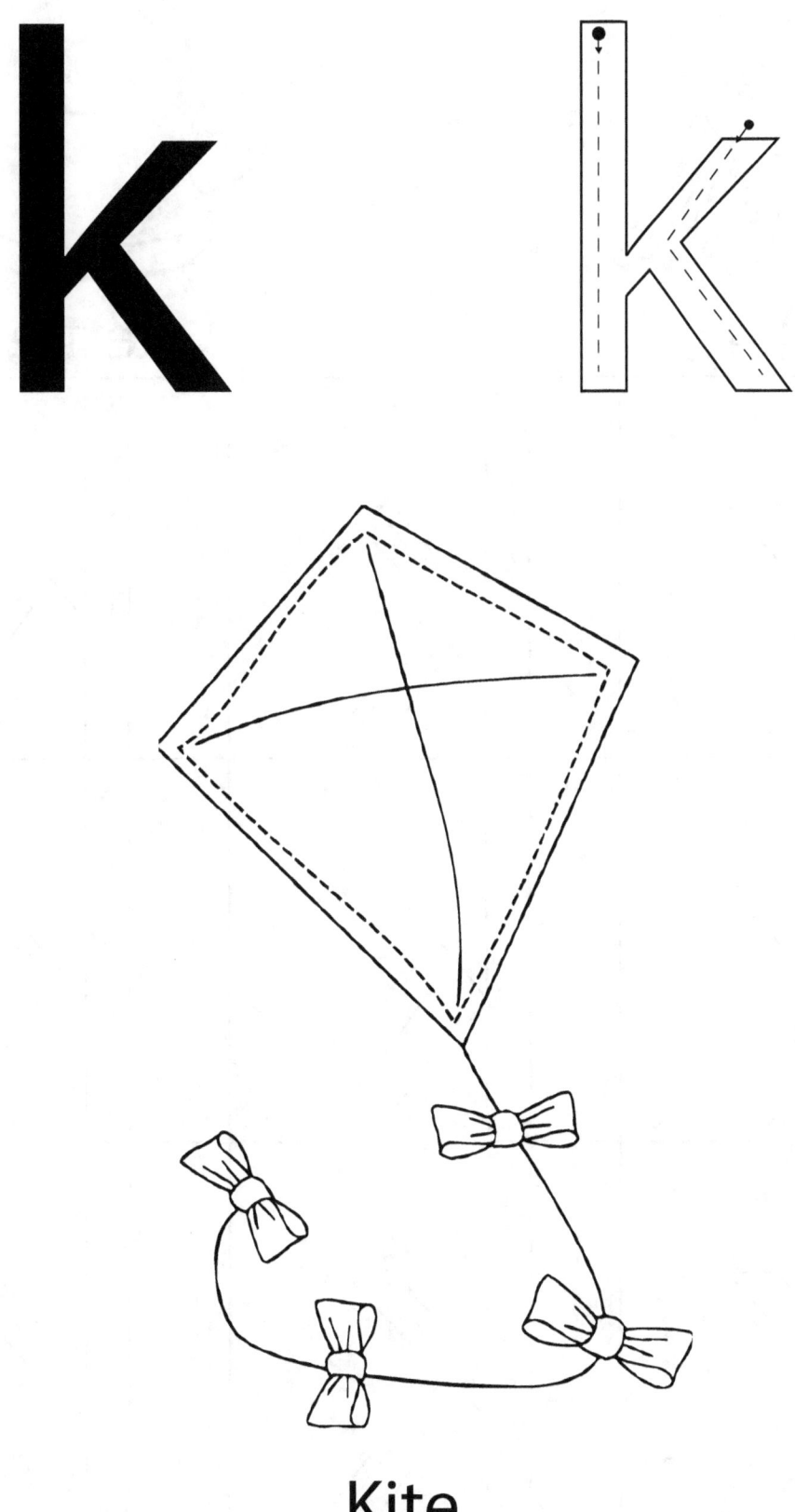

Kite

trace and color

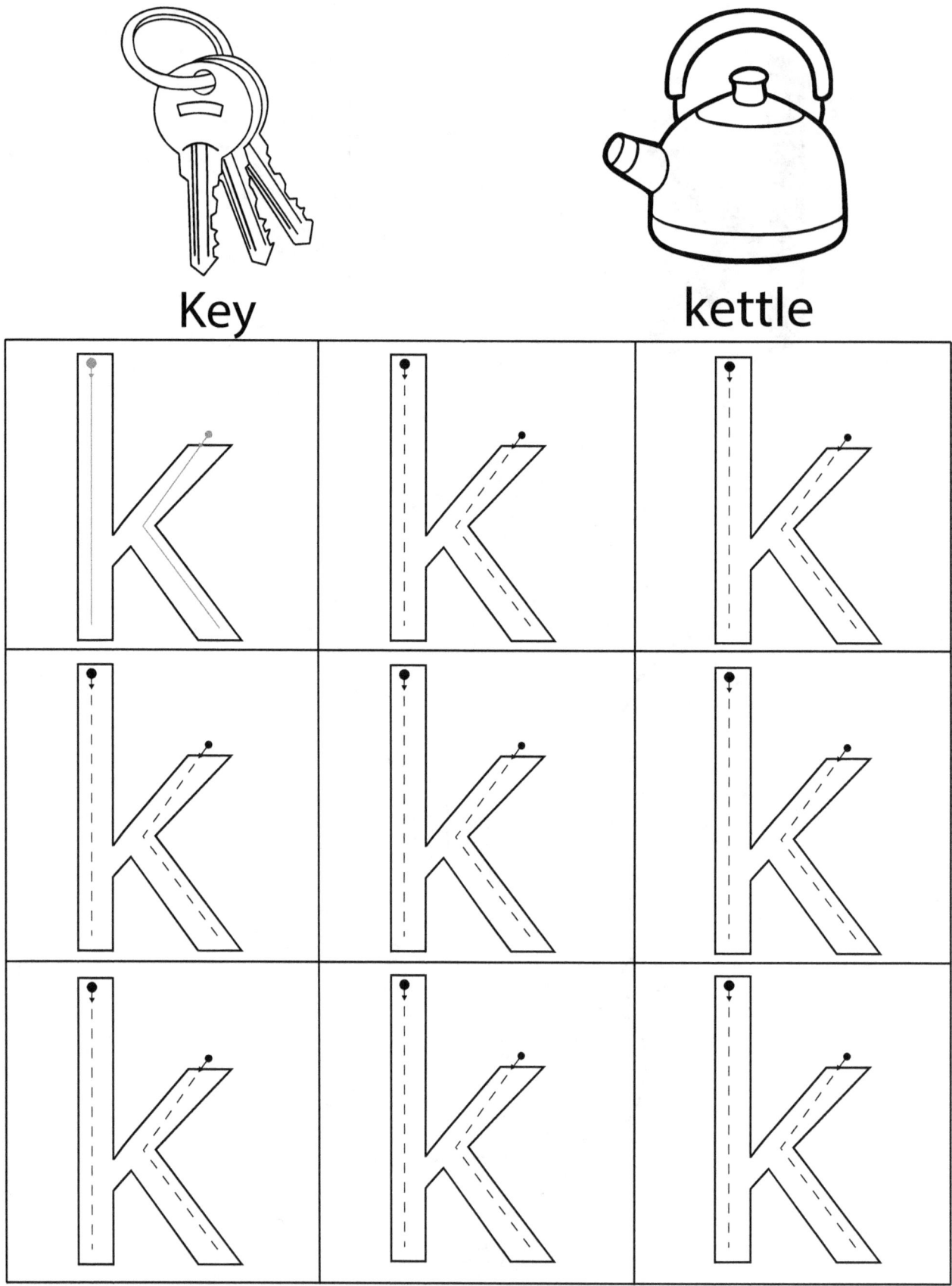

Key   kettle

trace and color

lamp

trace and color

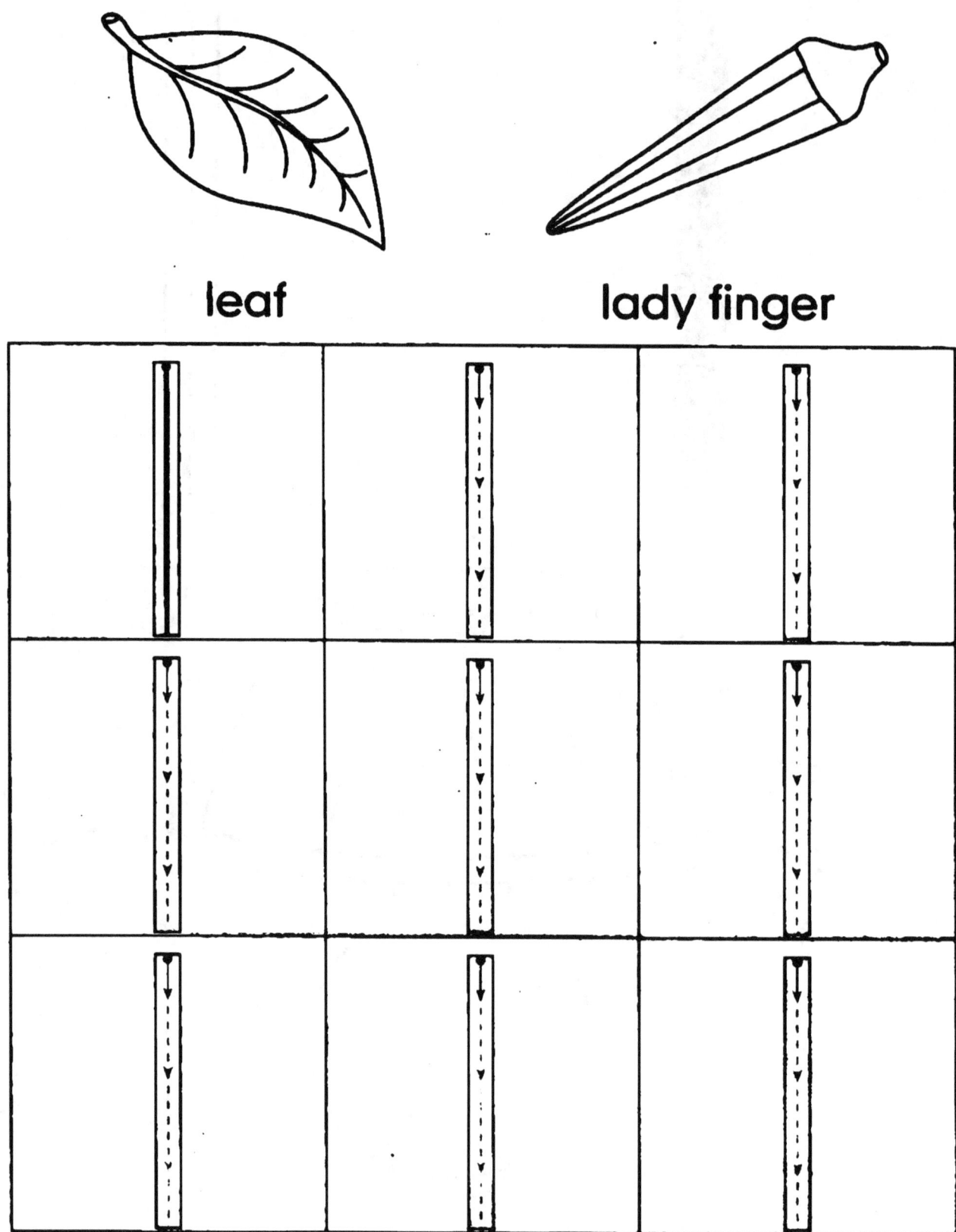

leaf   lady finger

trace and color

lock   lemon

write and color

lizard lion

trace and color

 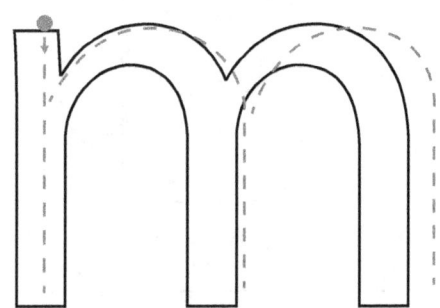

Mango

trace and color

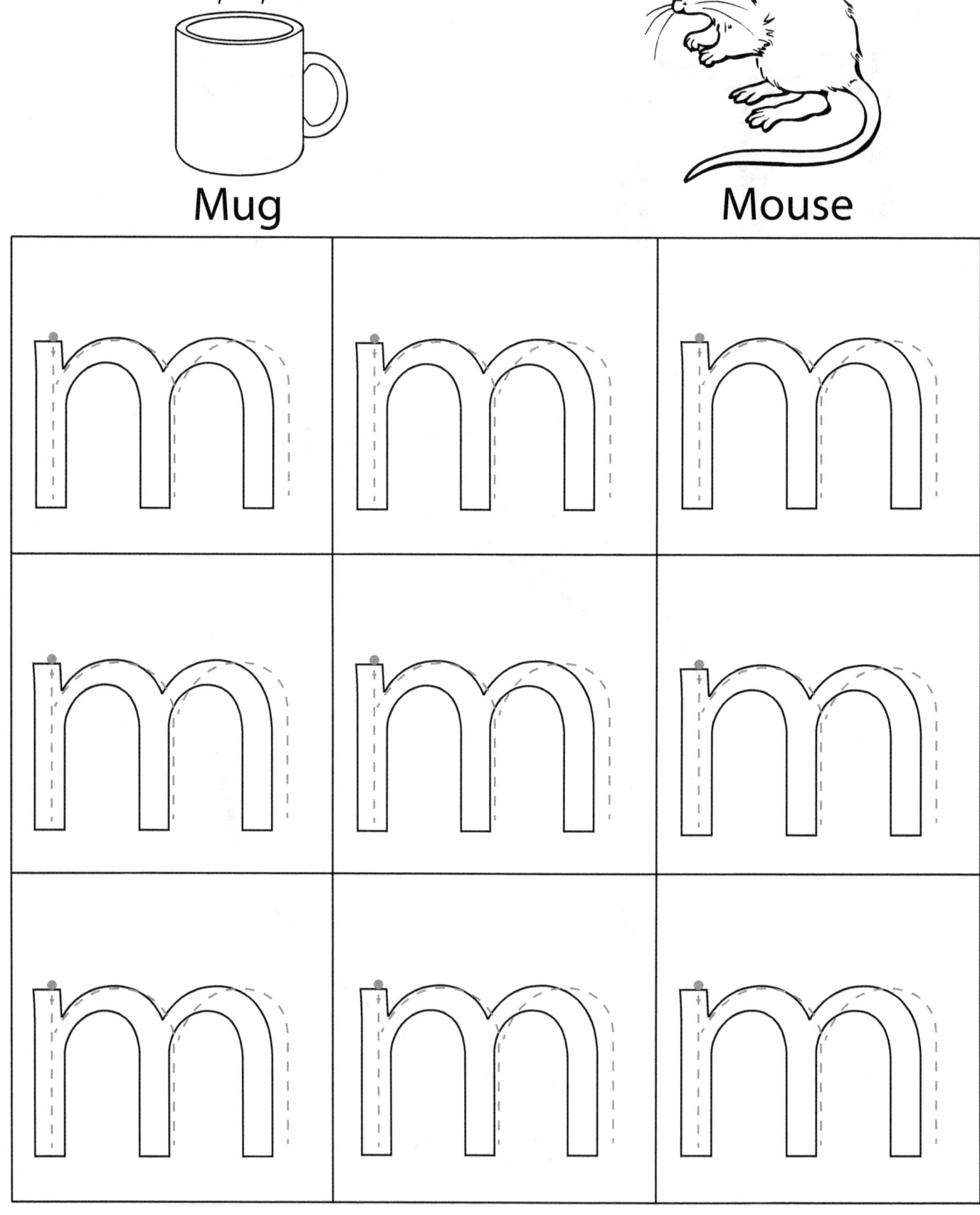

Mug Mouse

trace and color

Moon   Mask

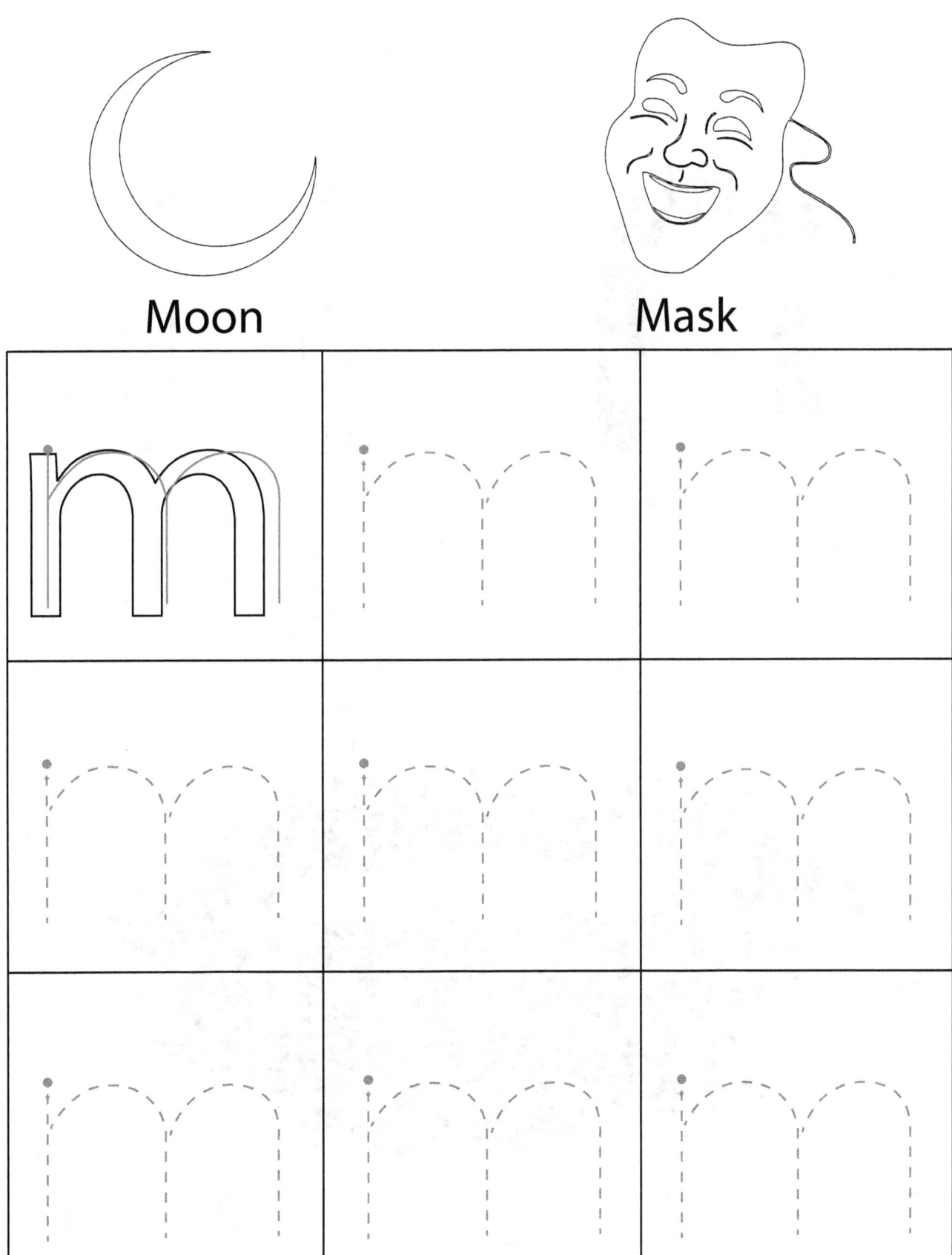

trace and color

 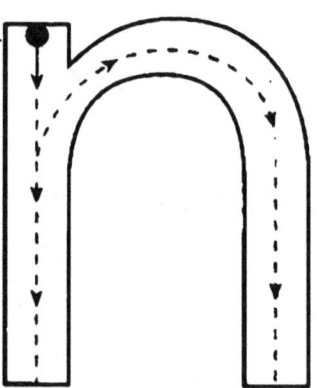

nest

trace and color

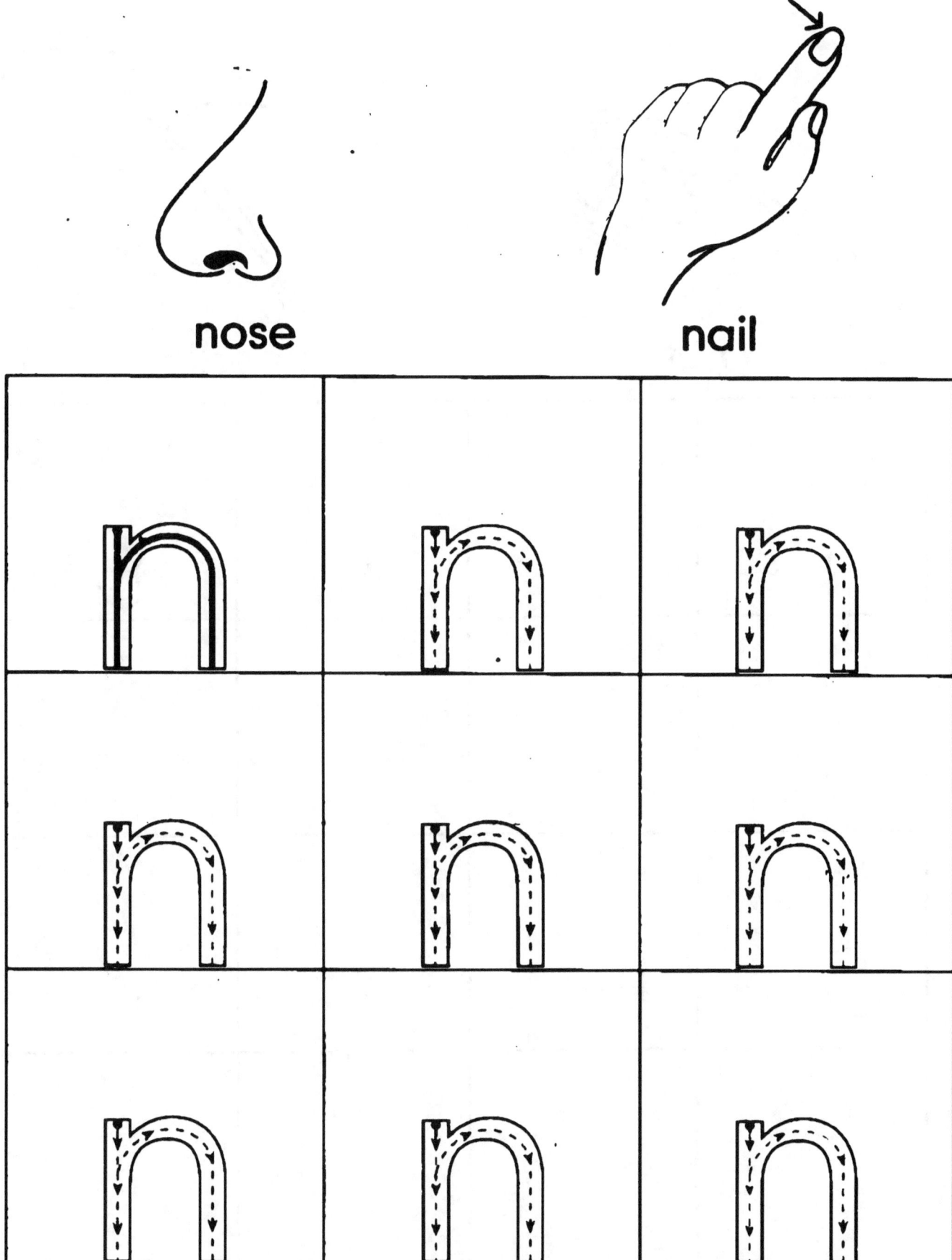

nose nail

write and color

 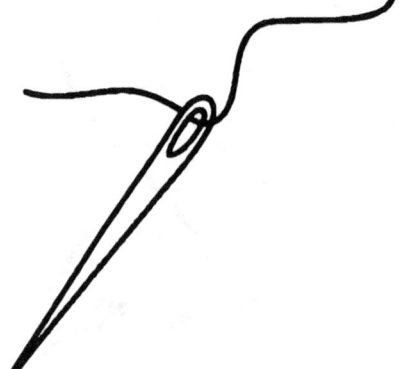

net   needle

trace and color

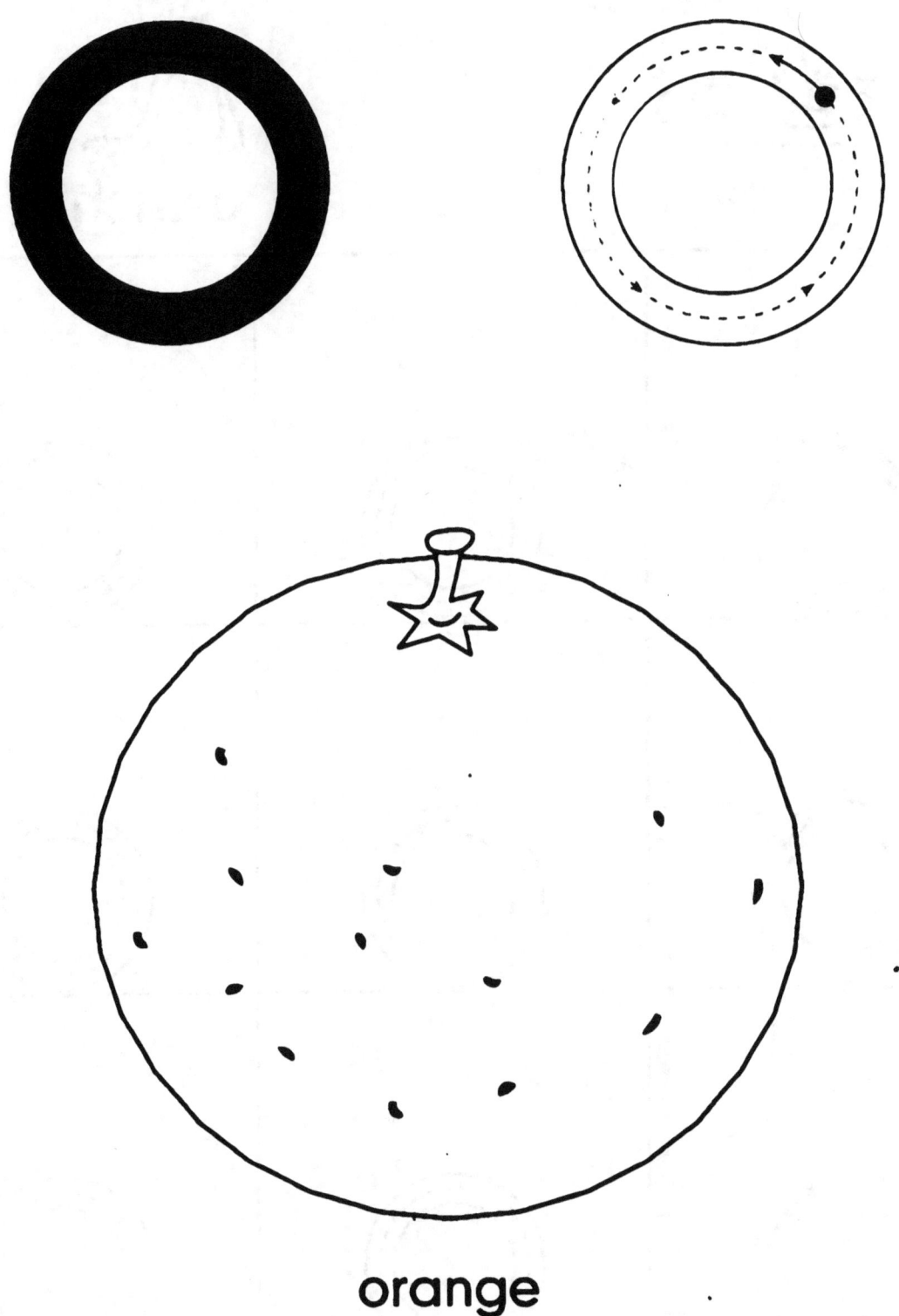

orange

trace and color

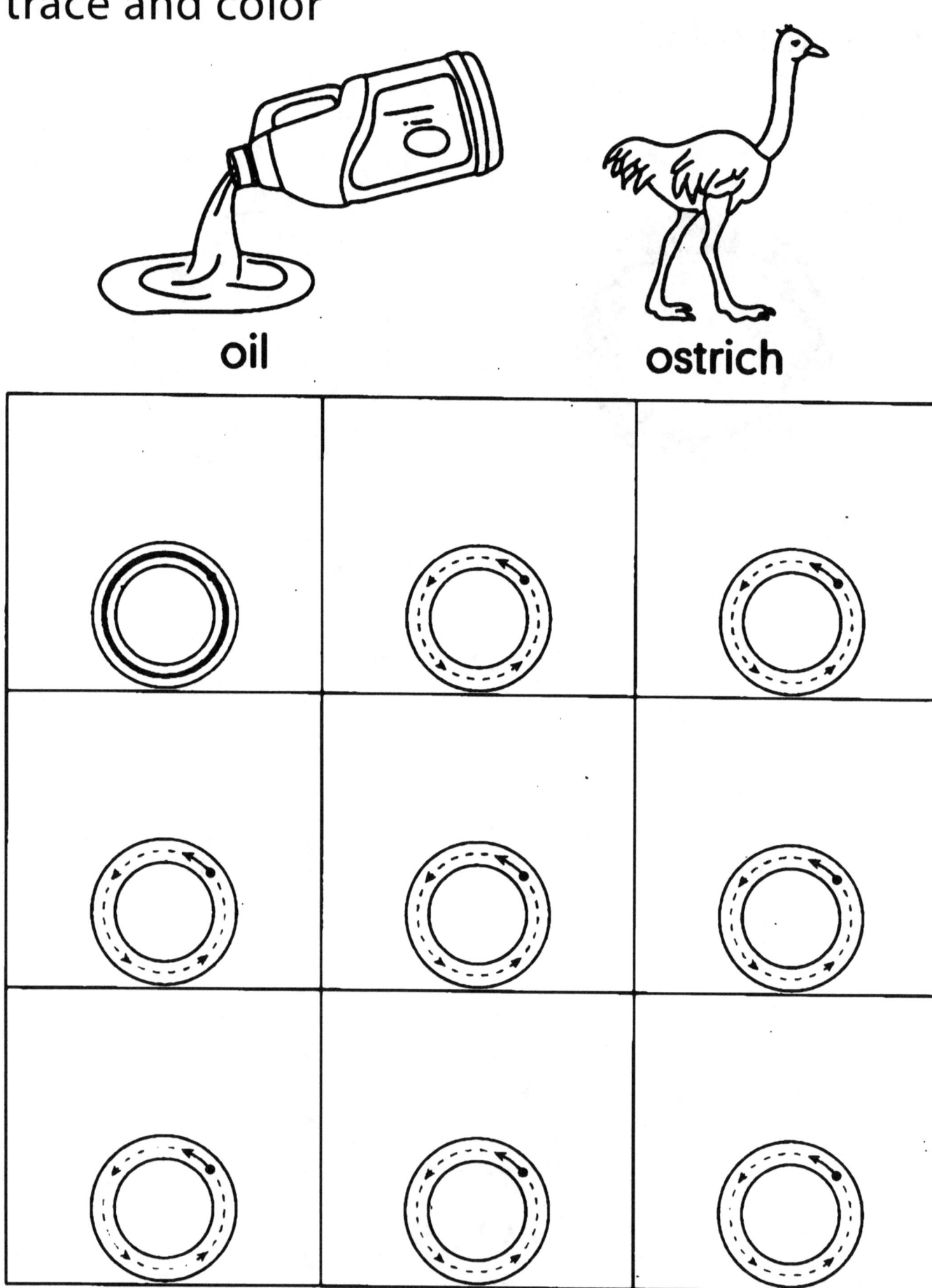

oil ostrich

write and color

omelette

ox

trace and color

pigeon

trace and color

peas   pear

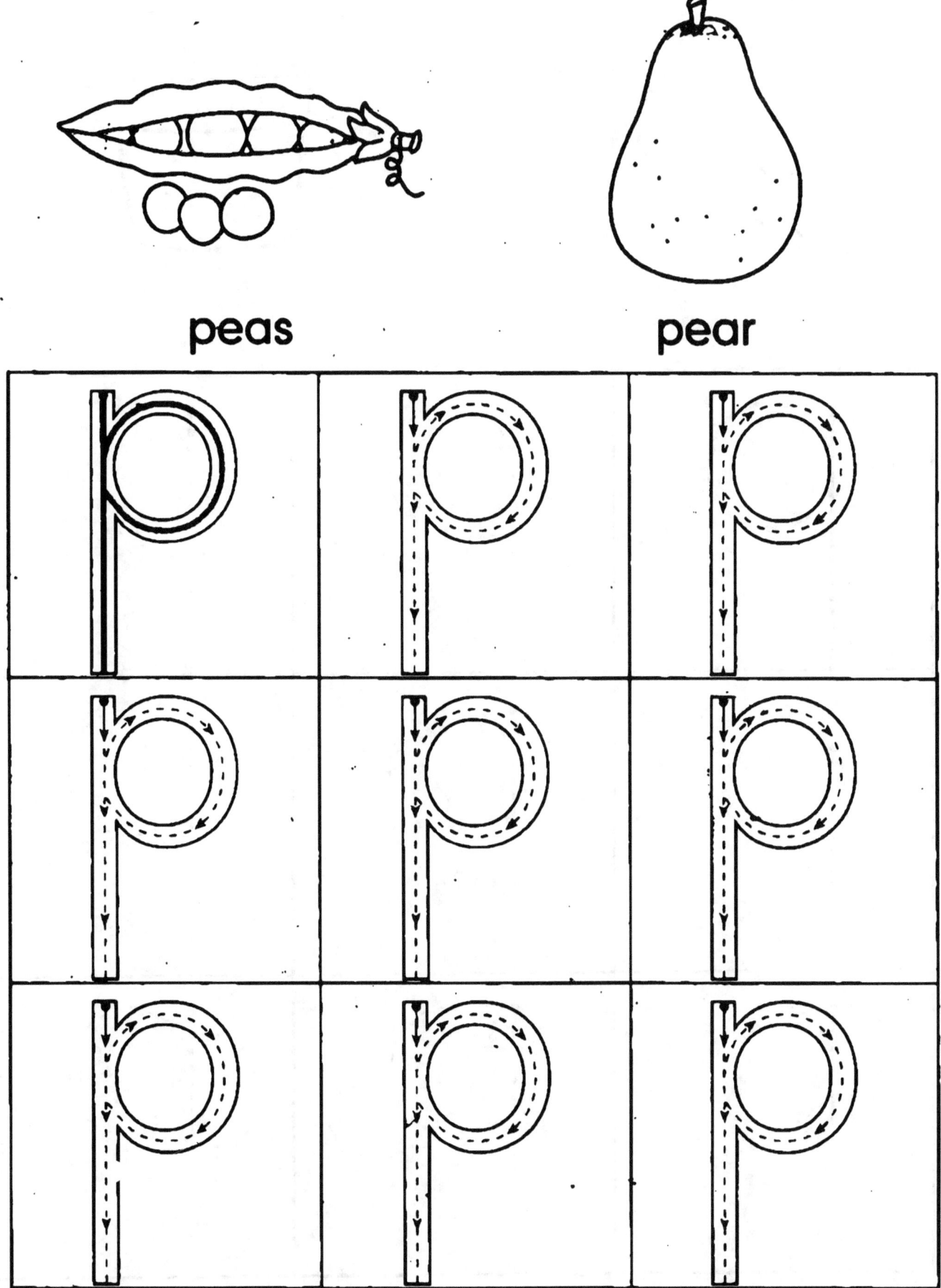

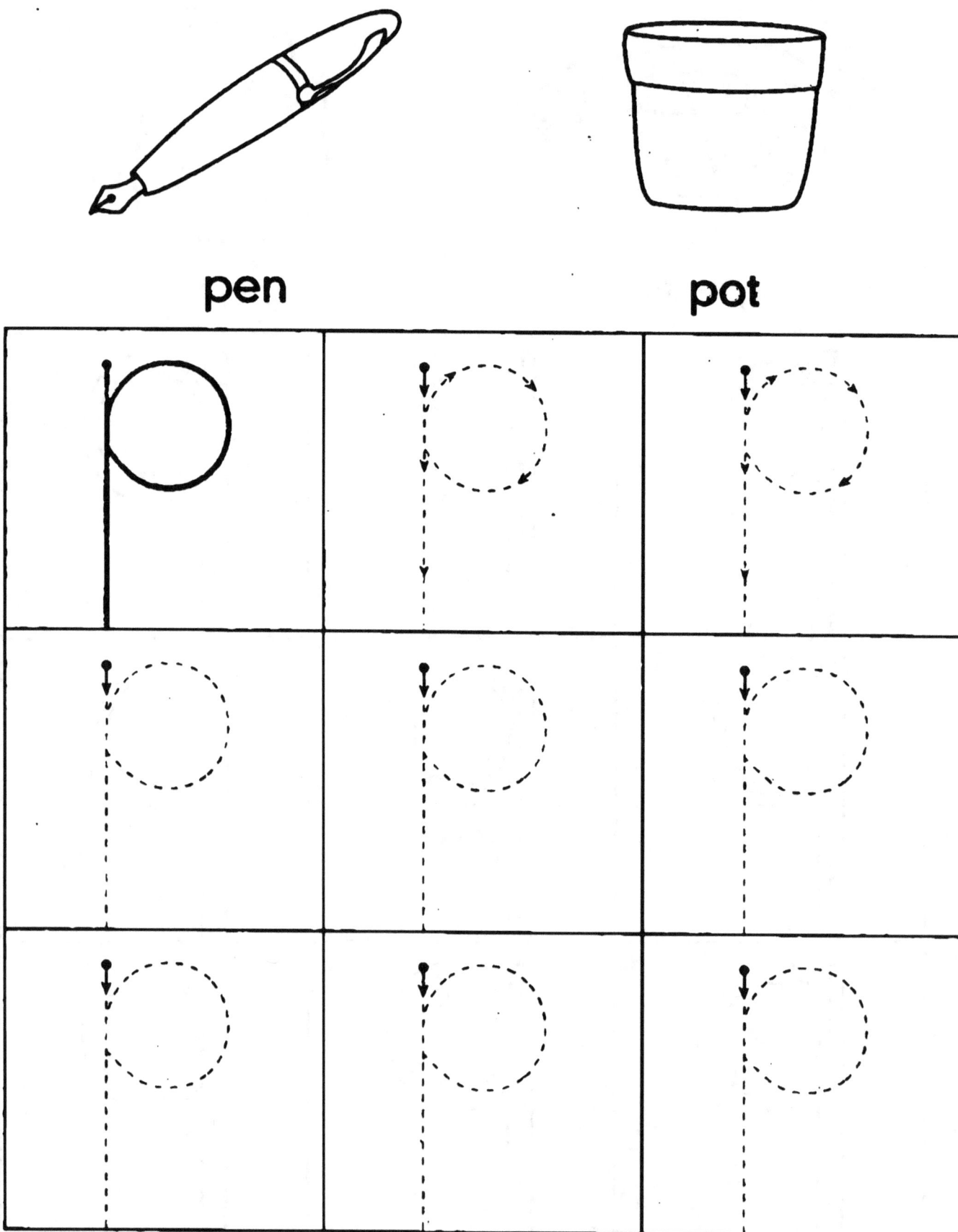

write and color

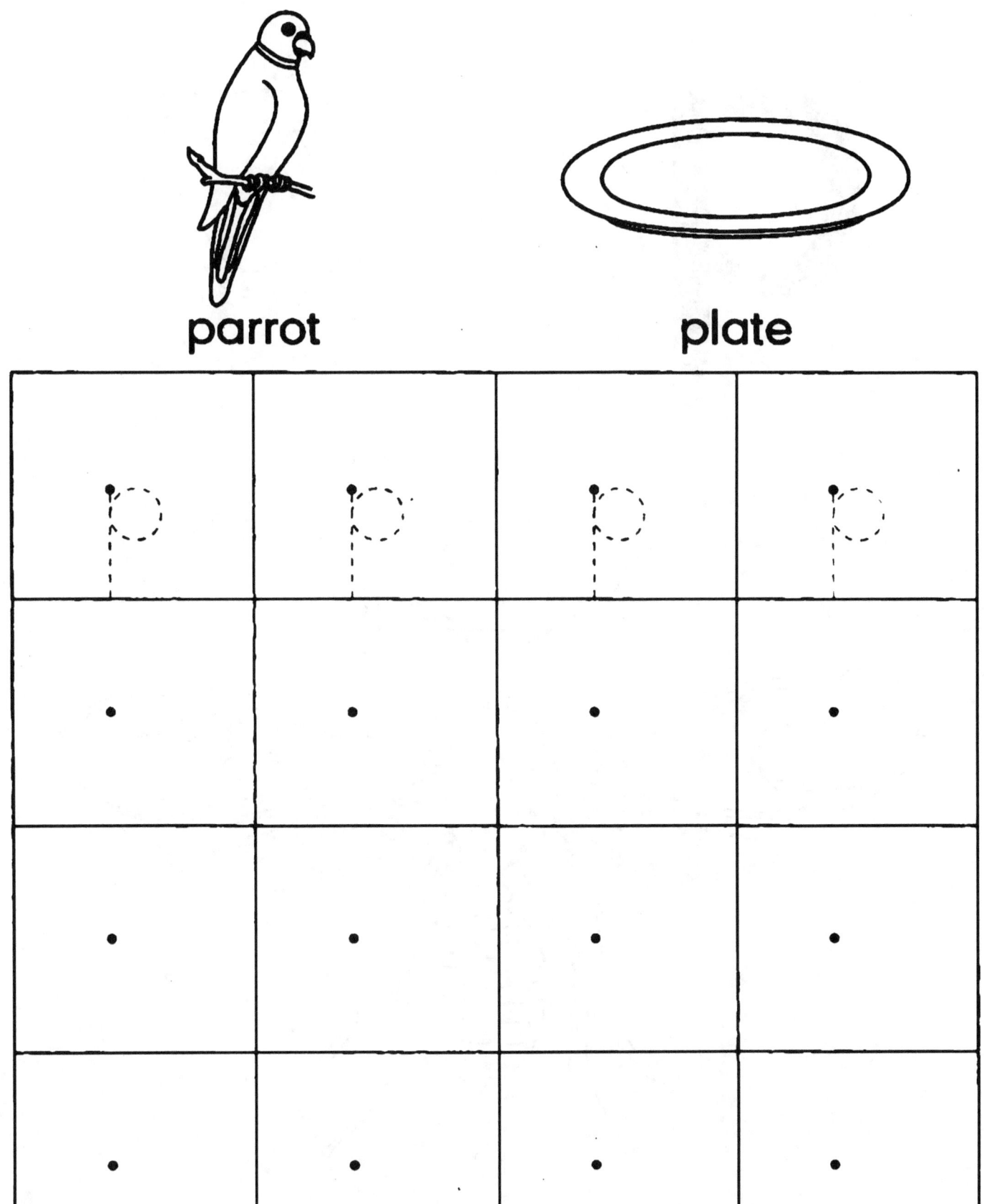

parrot plate

trace and color

 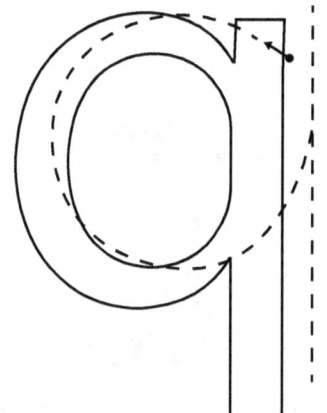

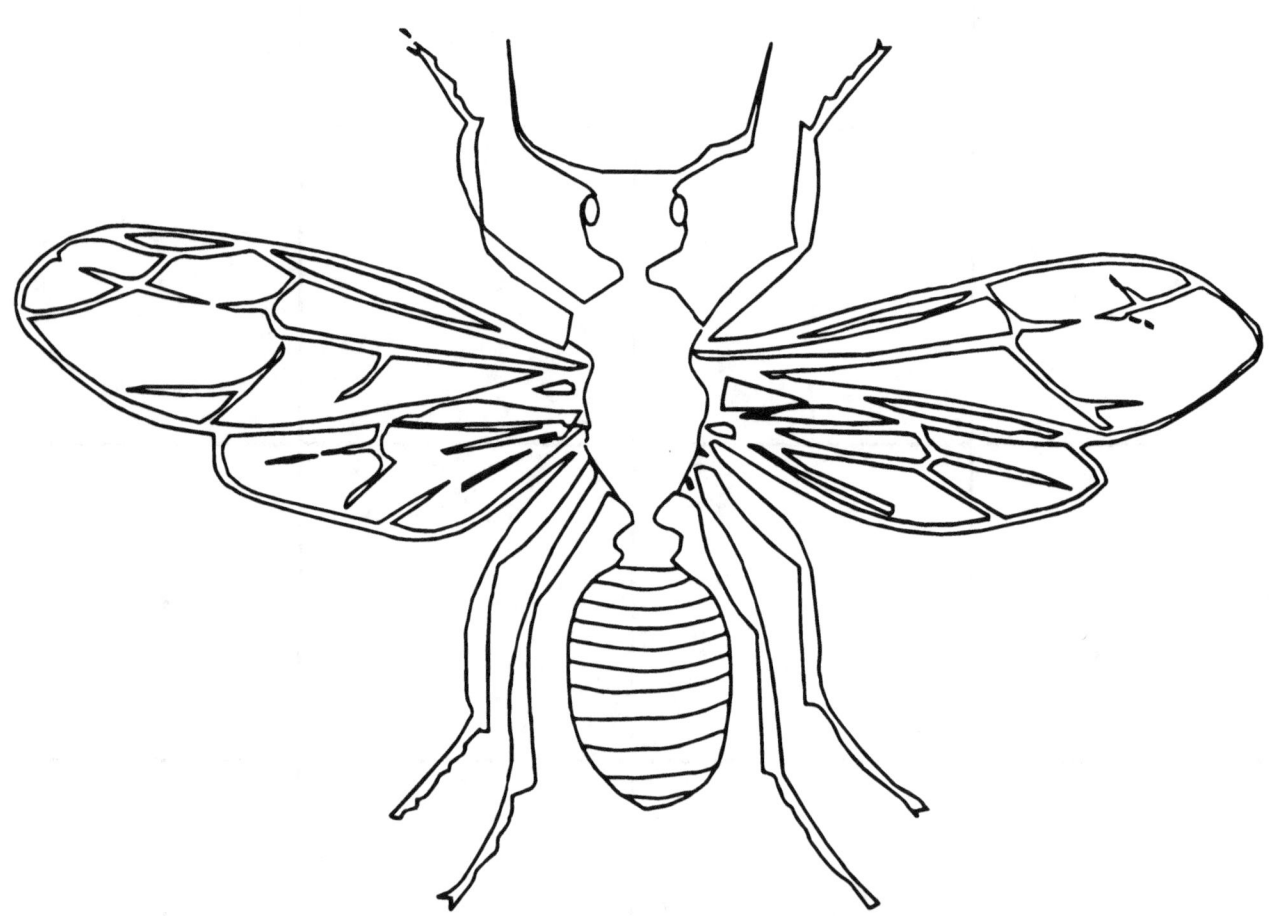

Queenant

trace and color

Quilt   Quill

trace and color

Quarter   Queen

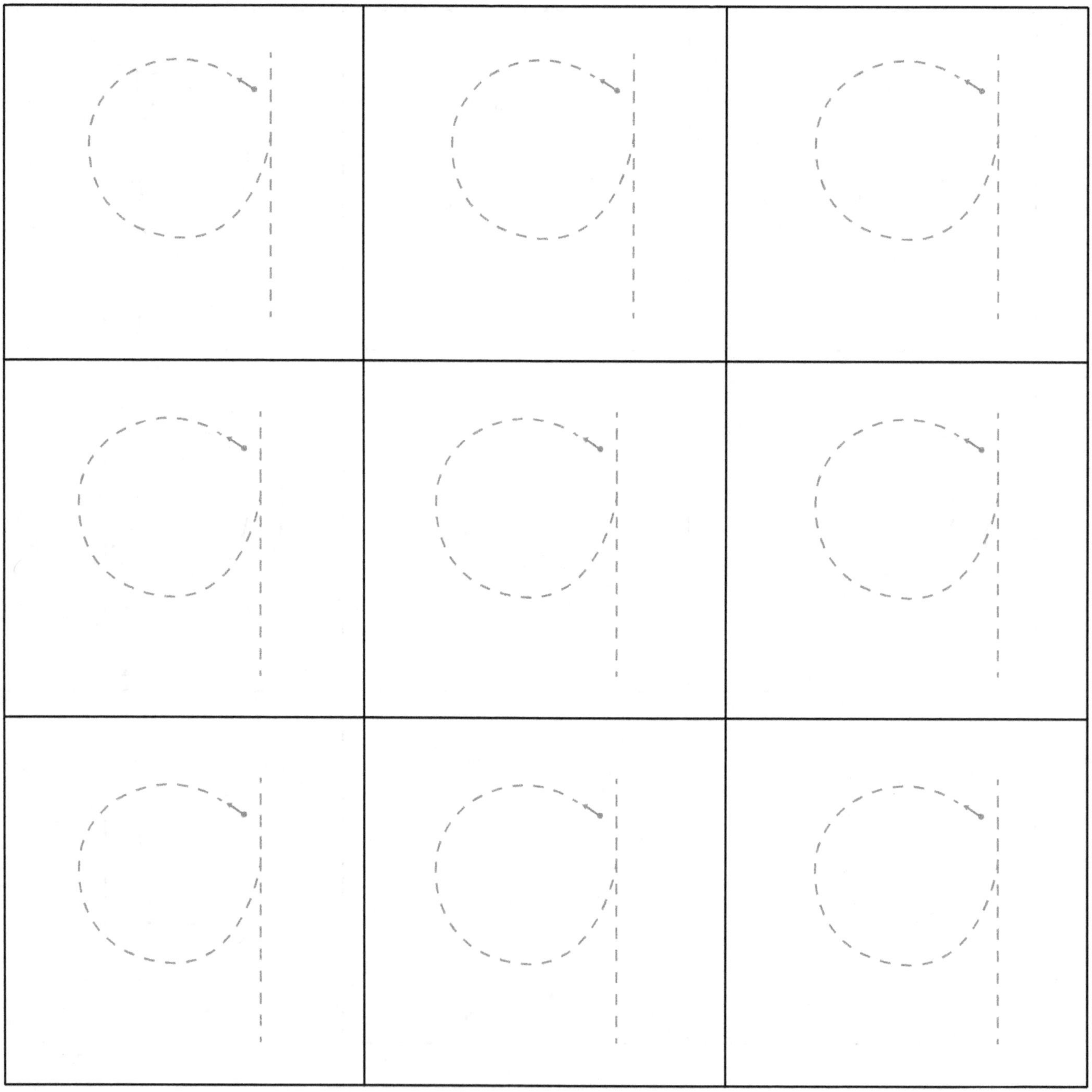

trace and color

rabbit

trace and color

rose   rat

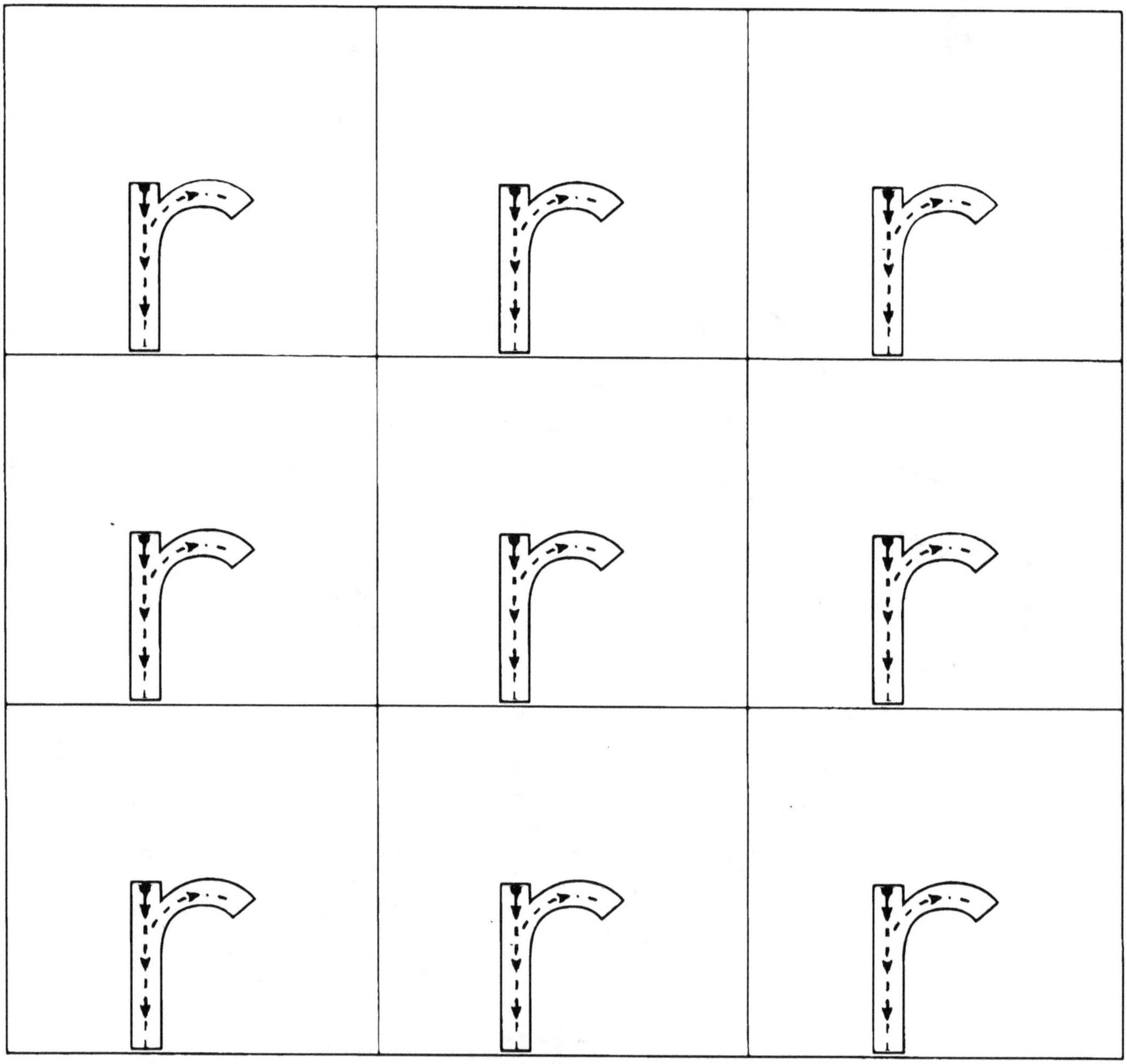

write and color

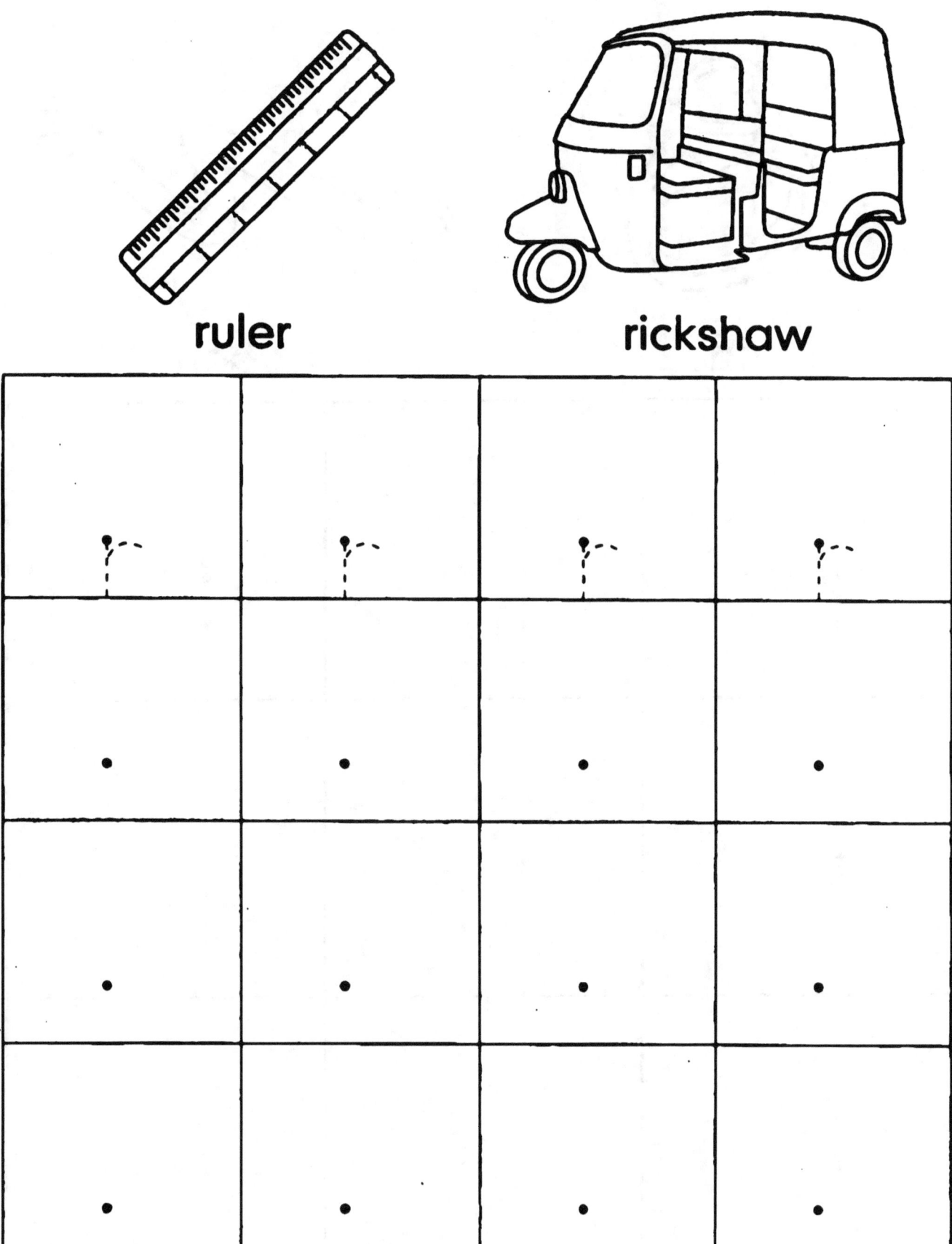

ruler   rickshaw

trace and color

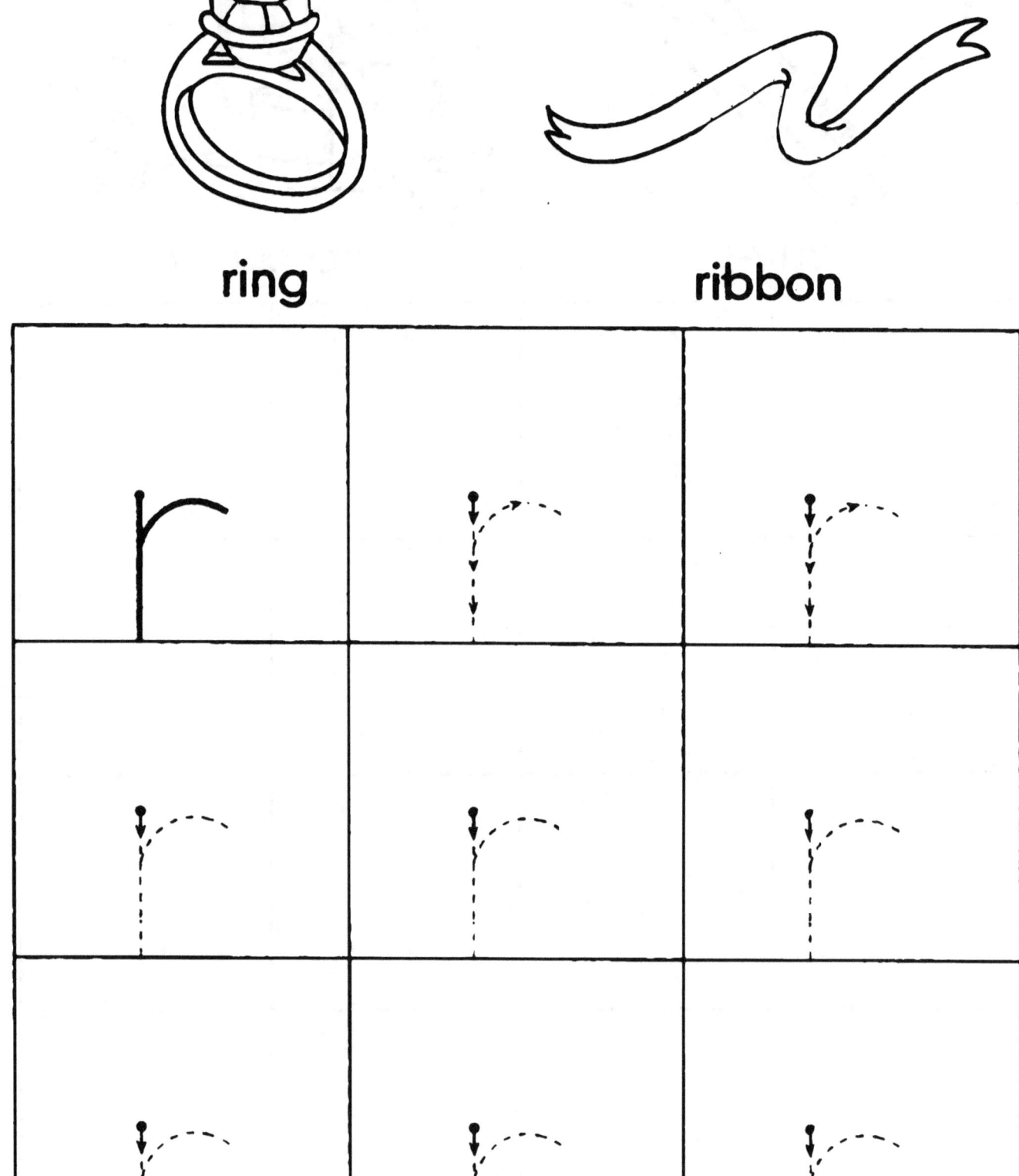

ring	ribbon

trace and color

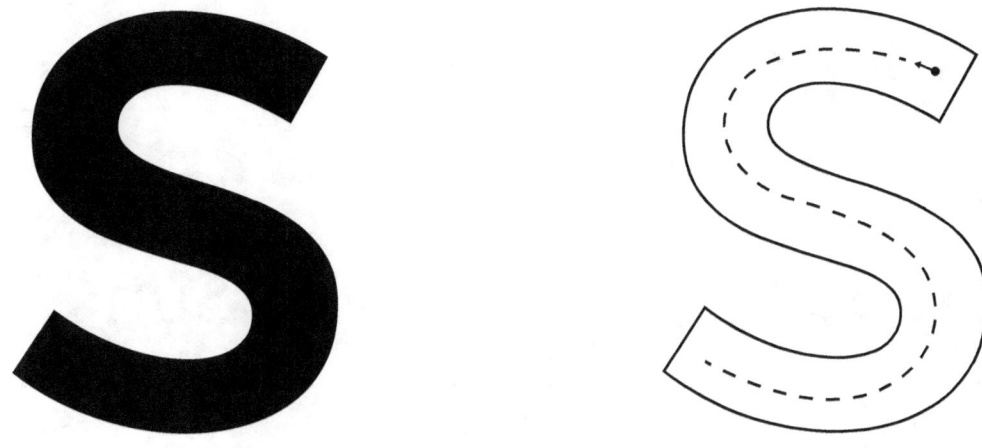

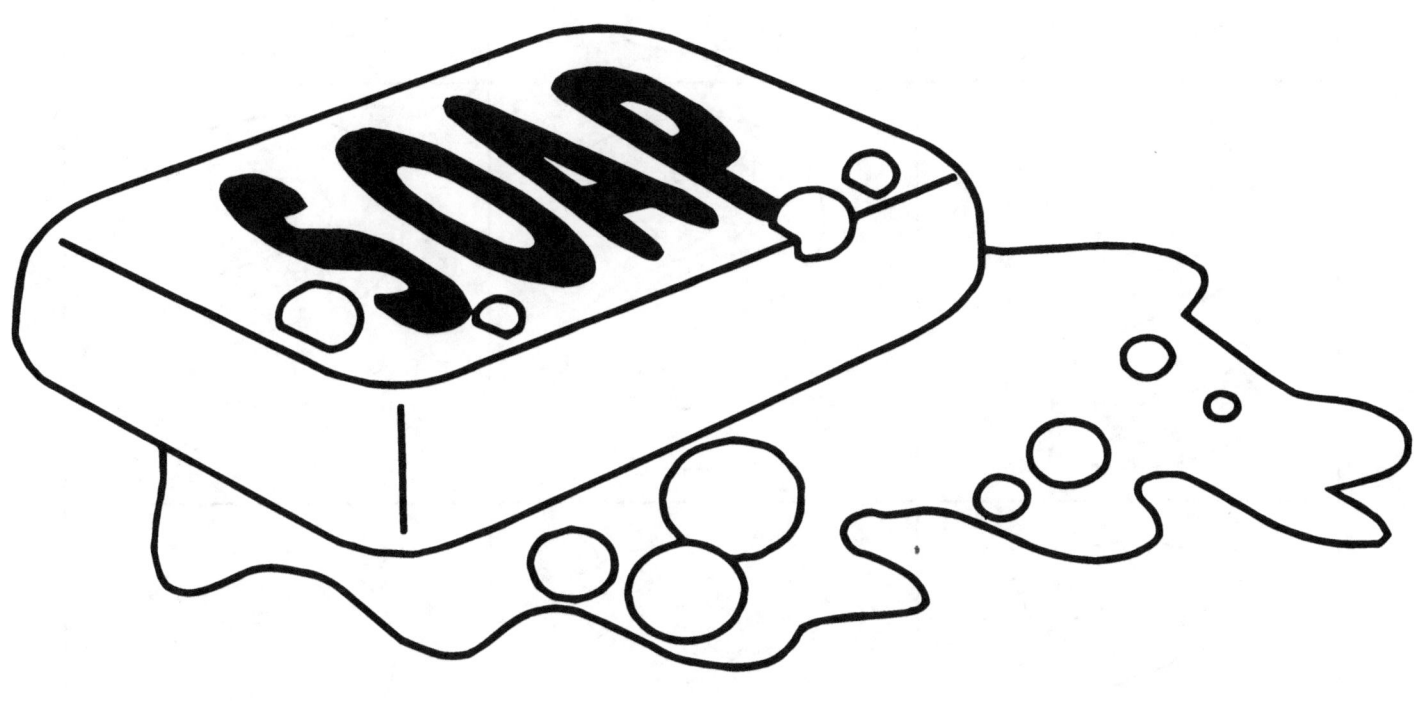

Soap

trace and color

Spoon   Sun

trace and color

Snake   Sofa

trace and color

t t

Tiger

trace and color

Telephone

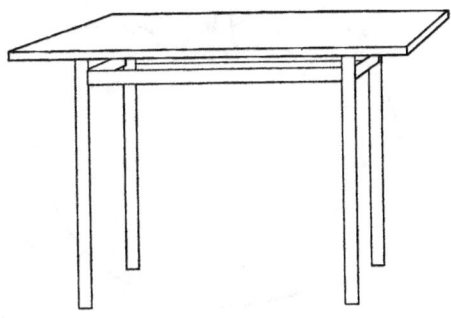
Table

trace and color

Tomato

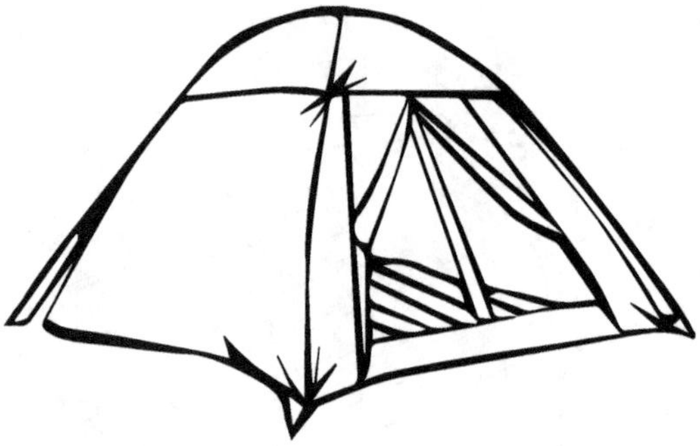

Tomato

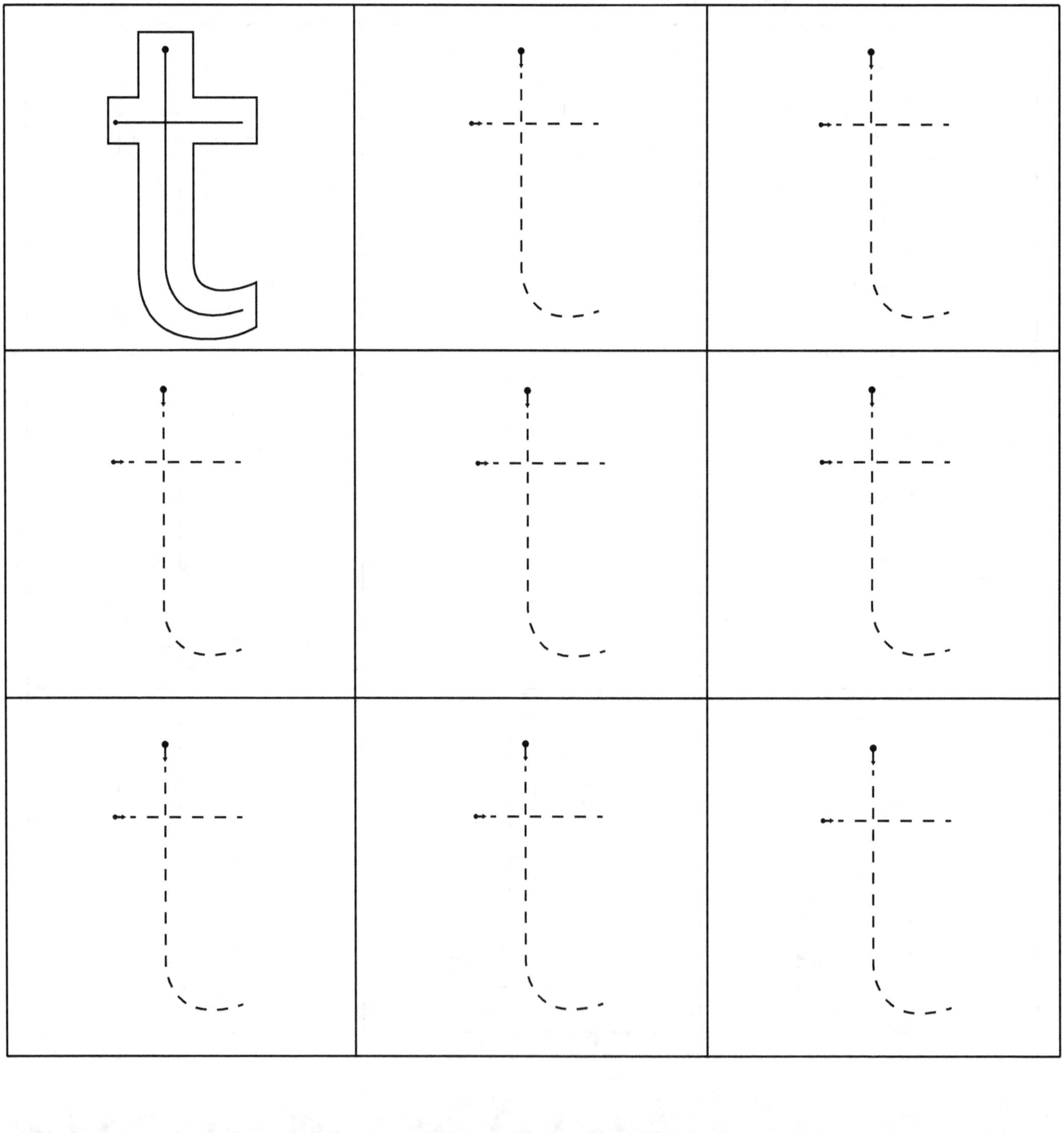

trace and color

Umbrella

trace and color

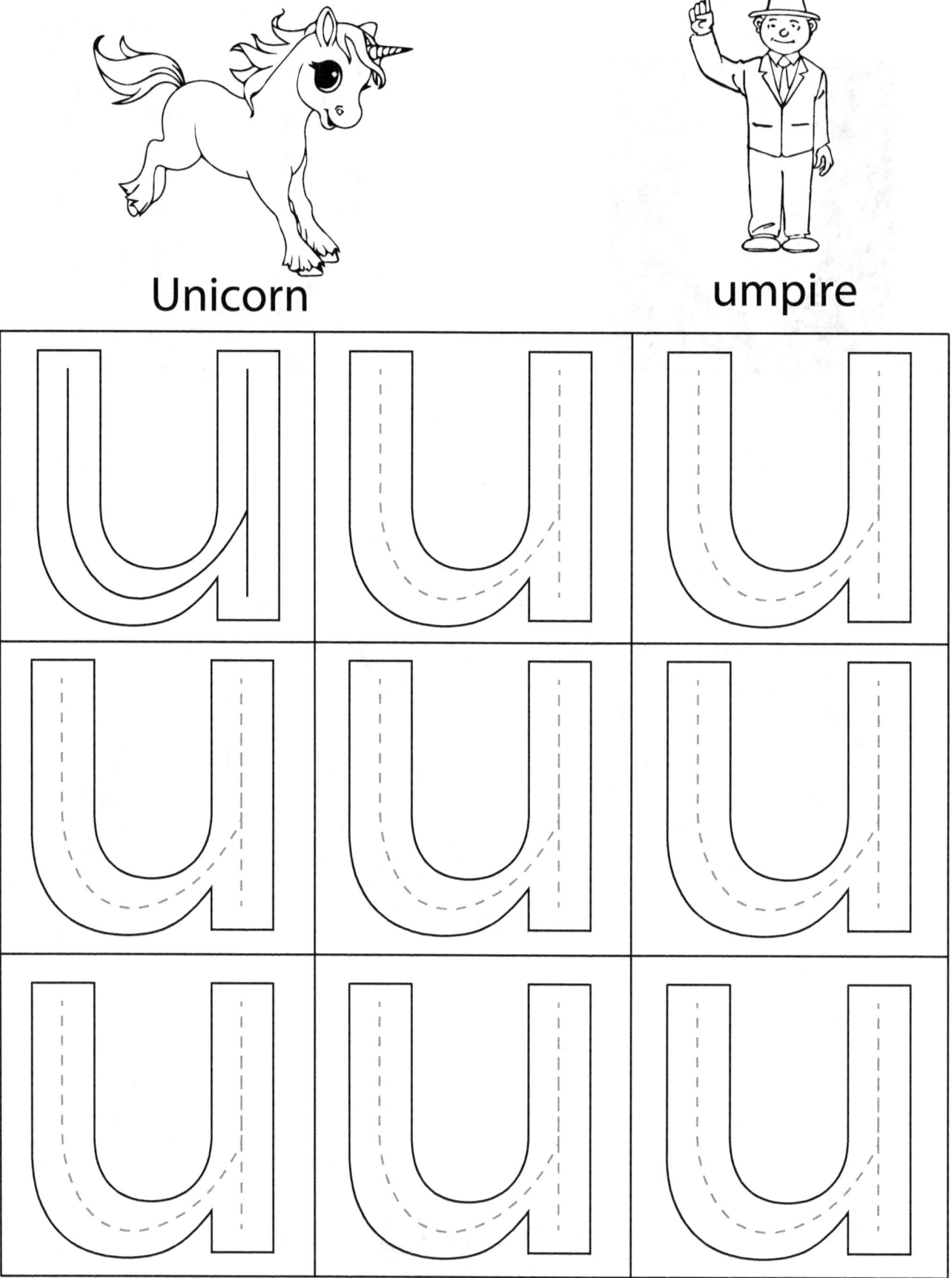

Unicorn umpire

trace and color

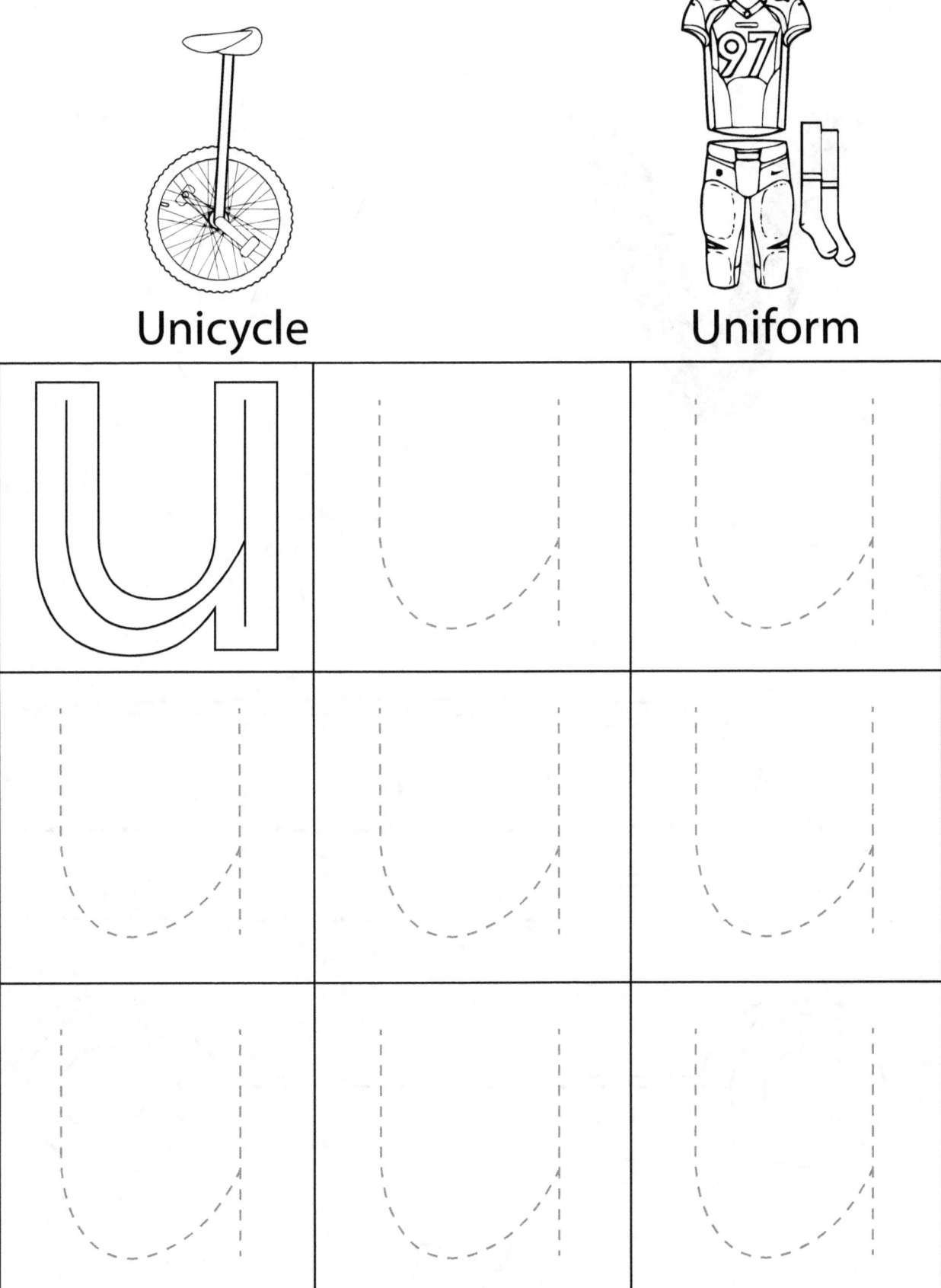

Unicycle   Uniform

trace and color

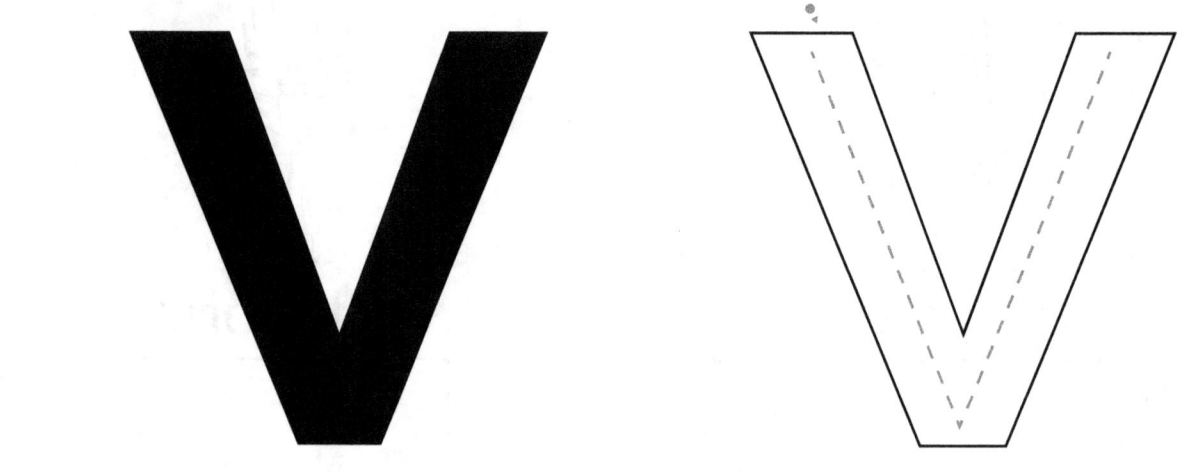

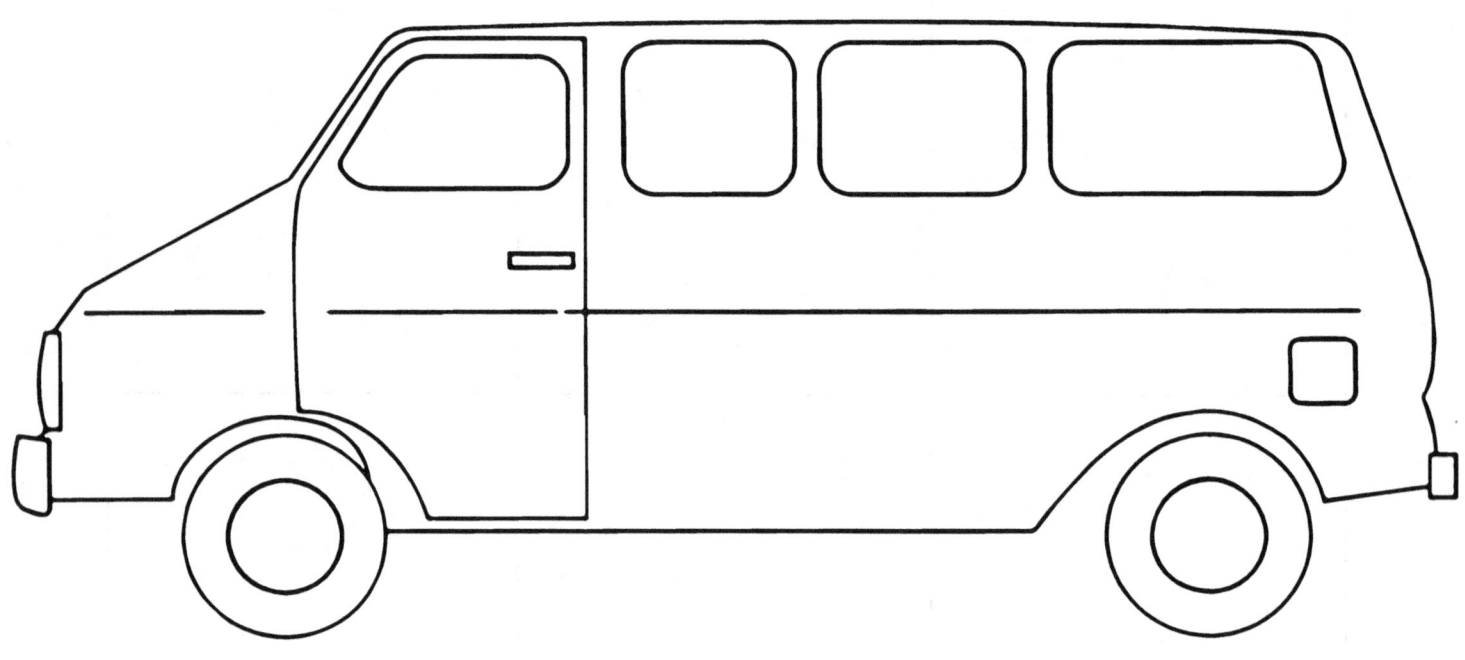

Van

trace and color

Vase

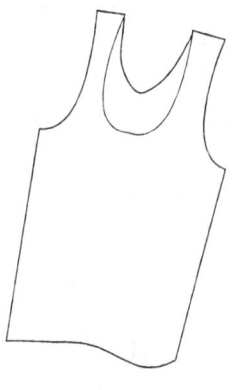

Vest

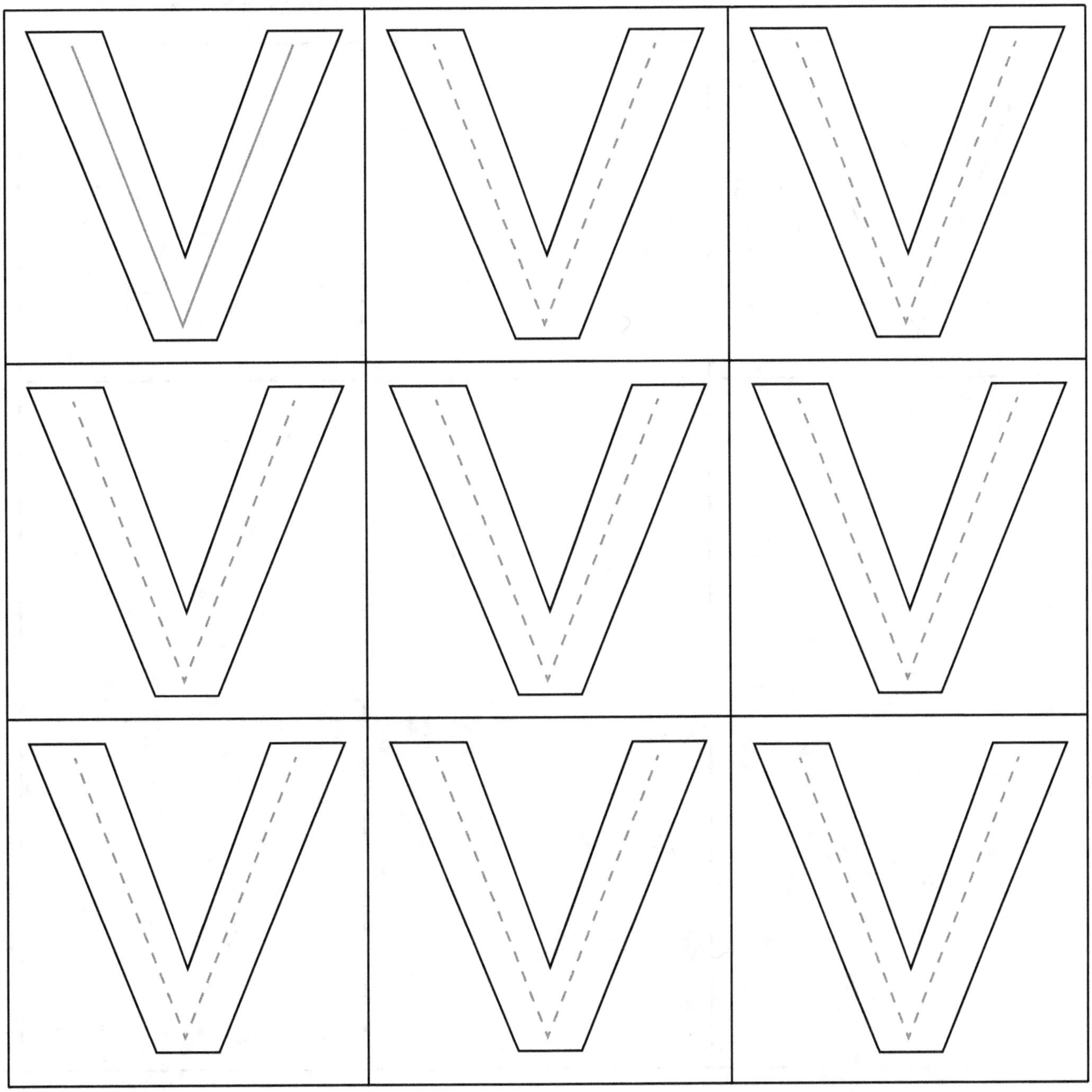

trace and color

Violin

Vegetables

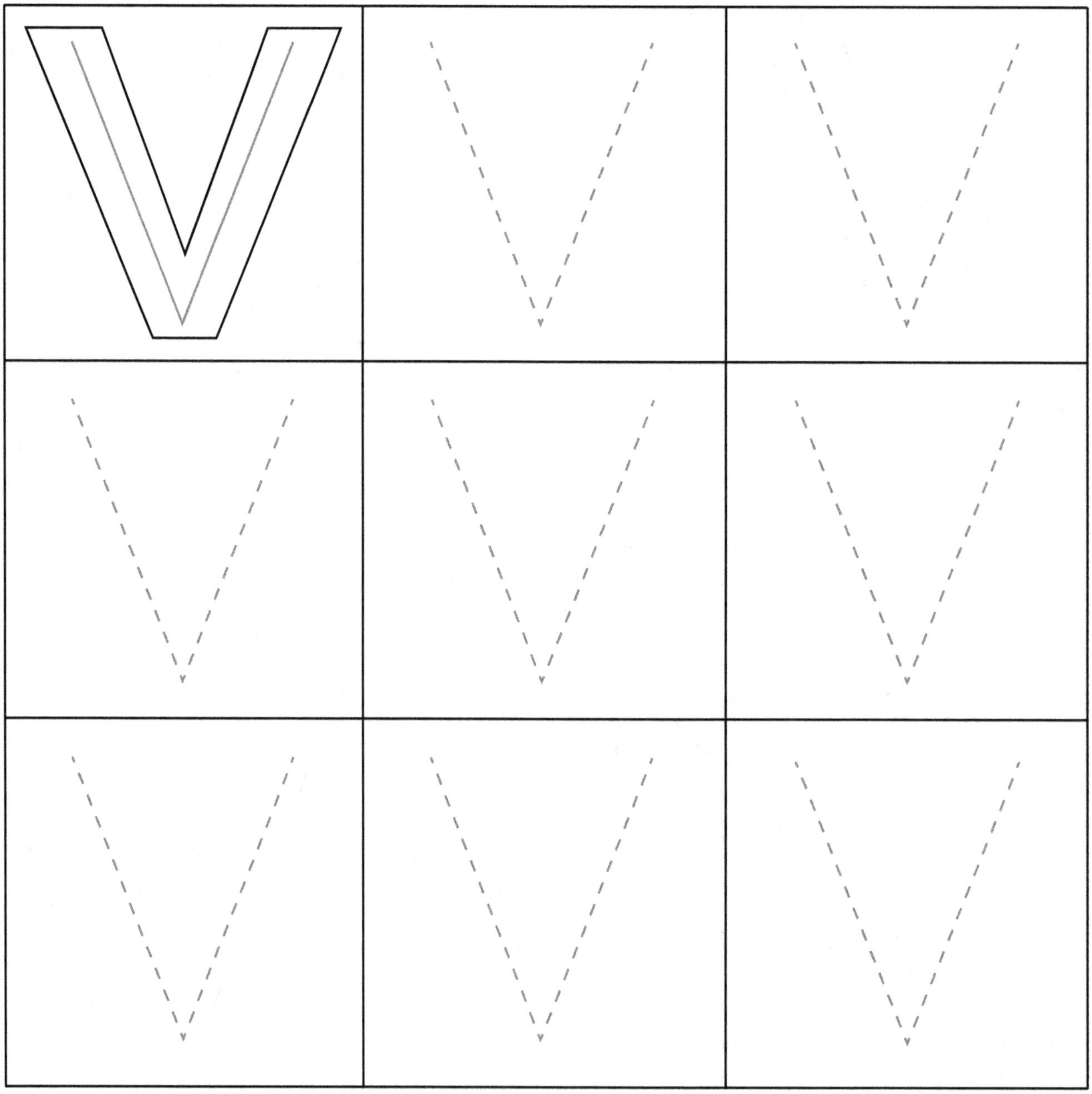

trace and color

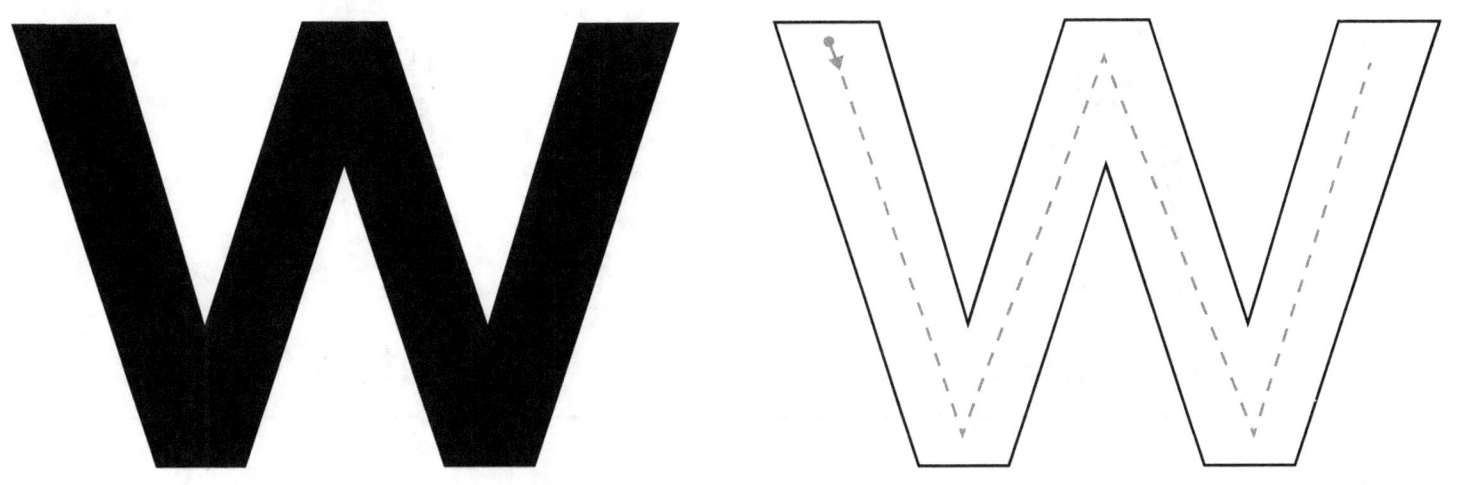

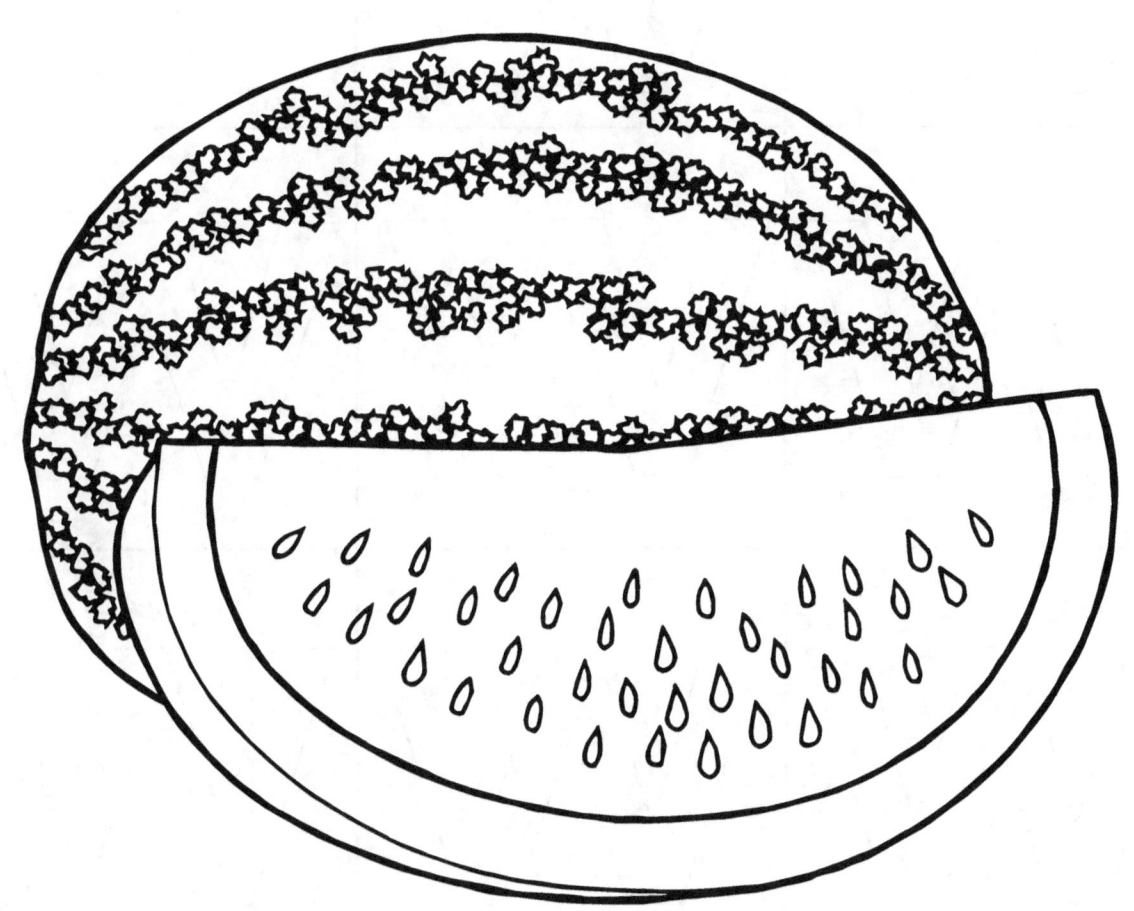

Watermelon

trace and color

Windmill					Watch

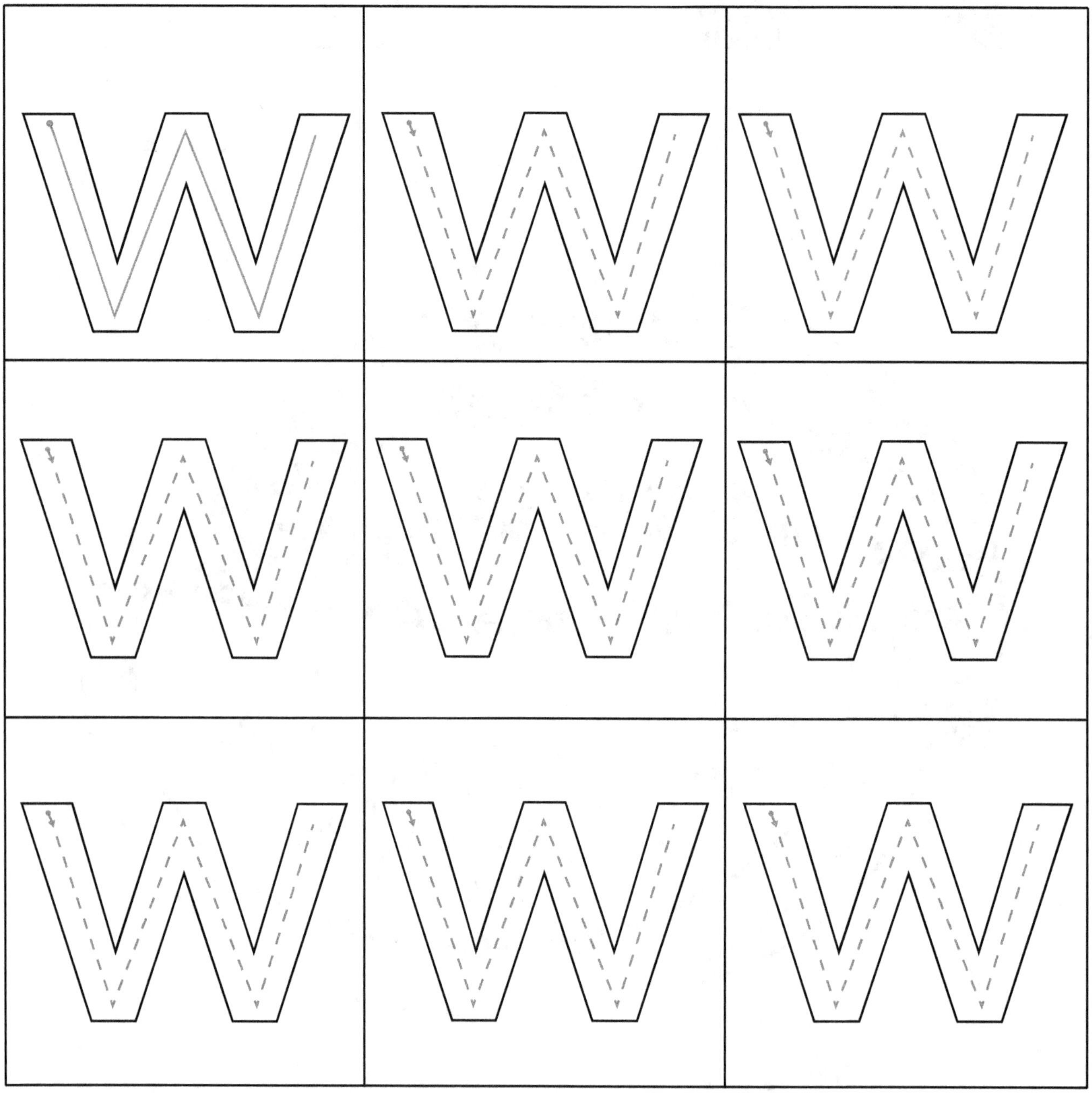

trace and color

Wand

Walrus

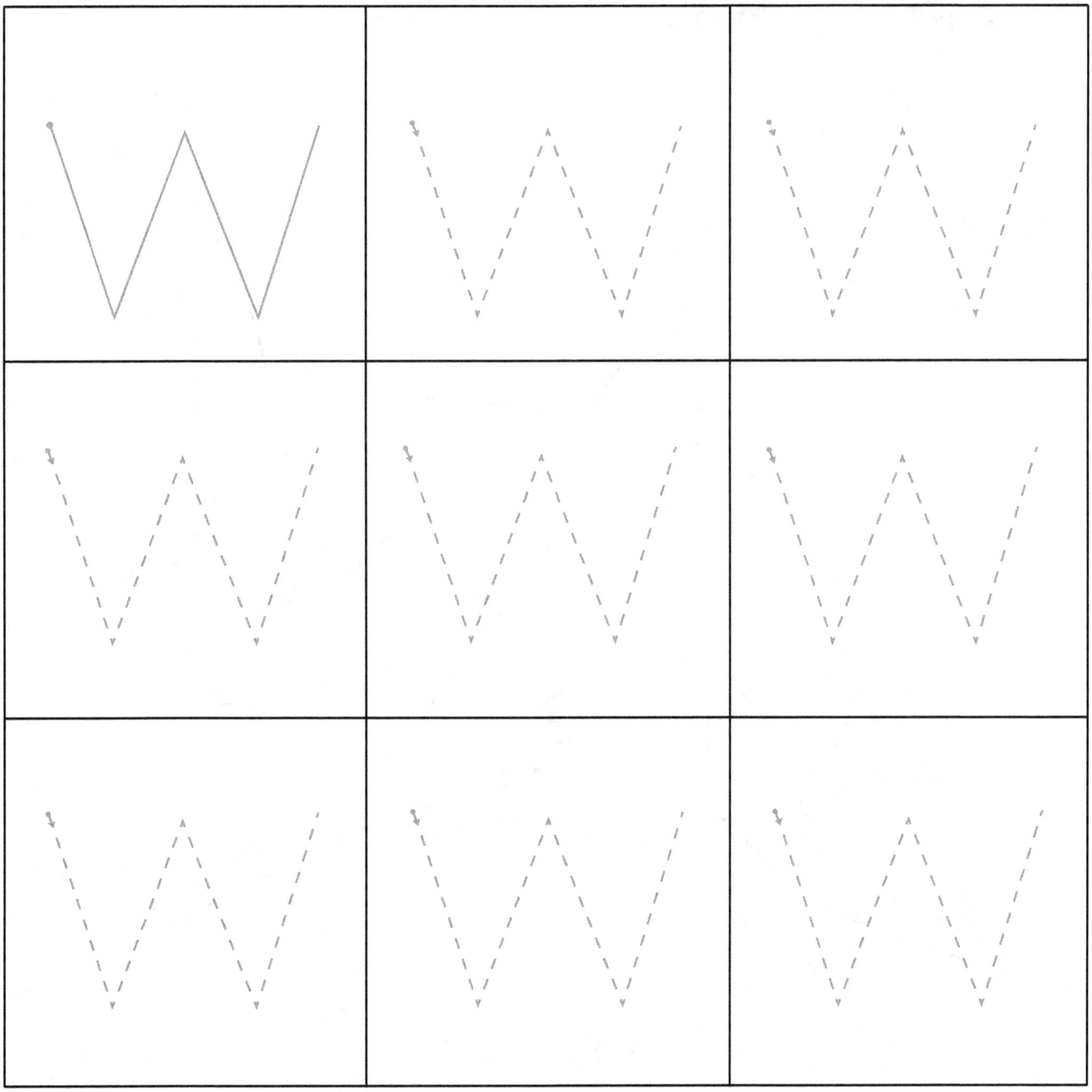

trace and color

X X

Xiphias

trace and color

Xylophone	Ximenia

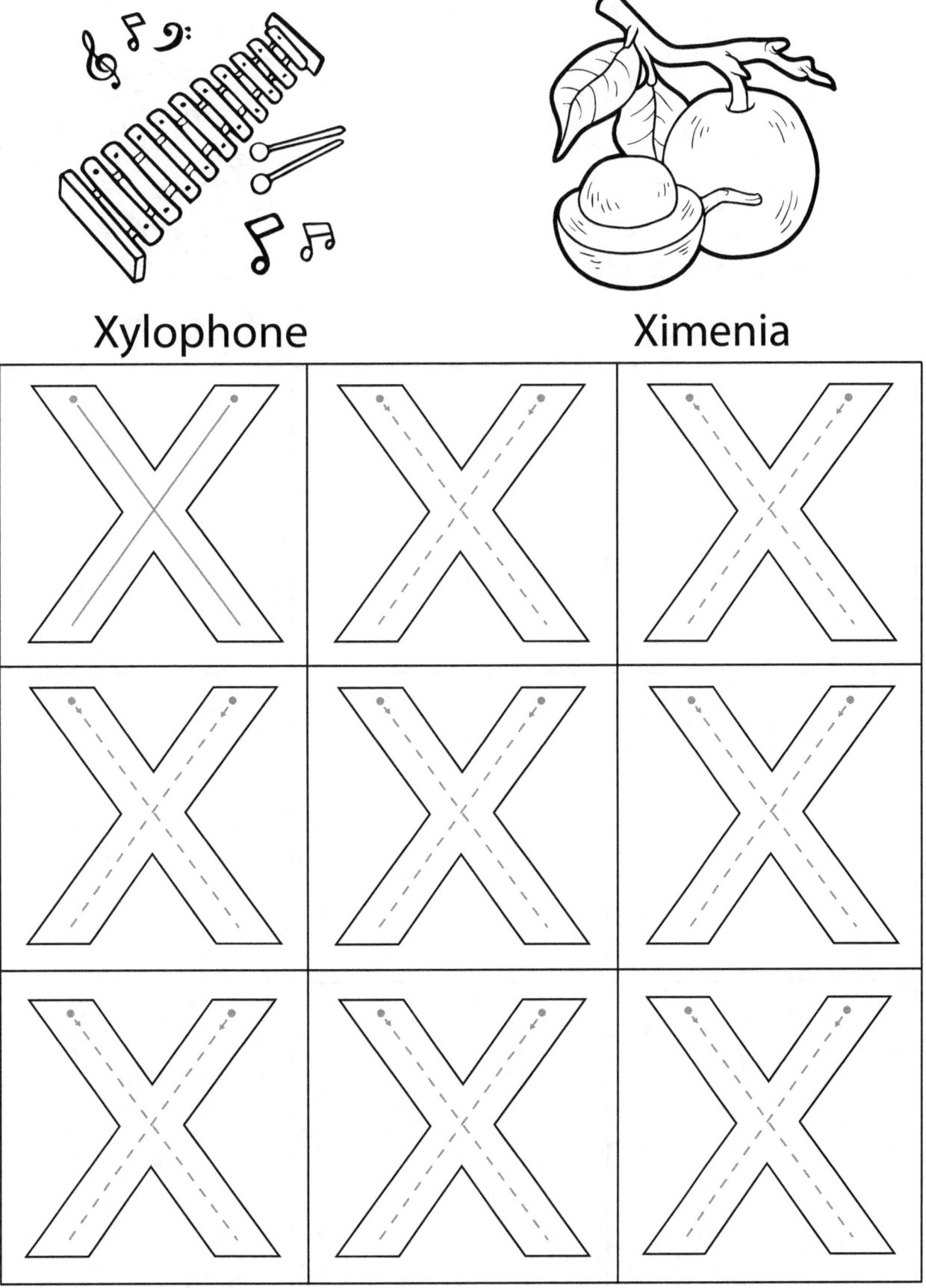

trace and color

xerus

Xmas tree

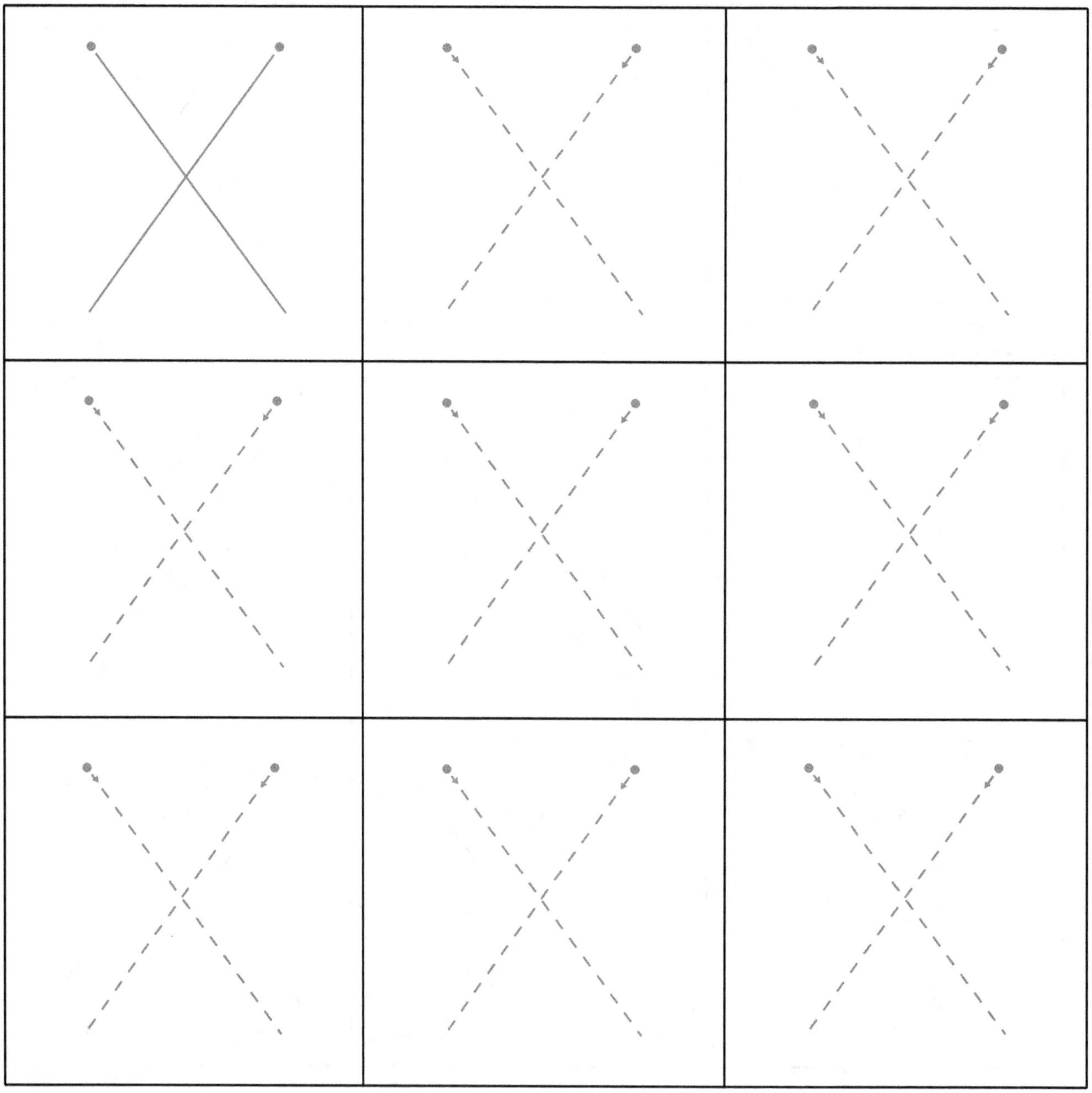

trace and color

y y

Yacht

trace and color

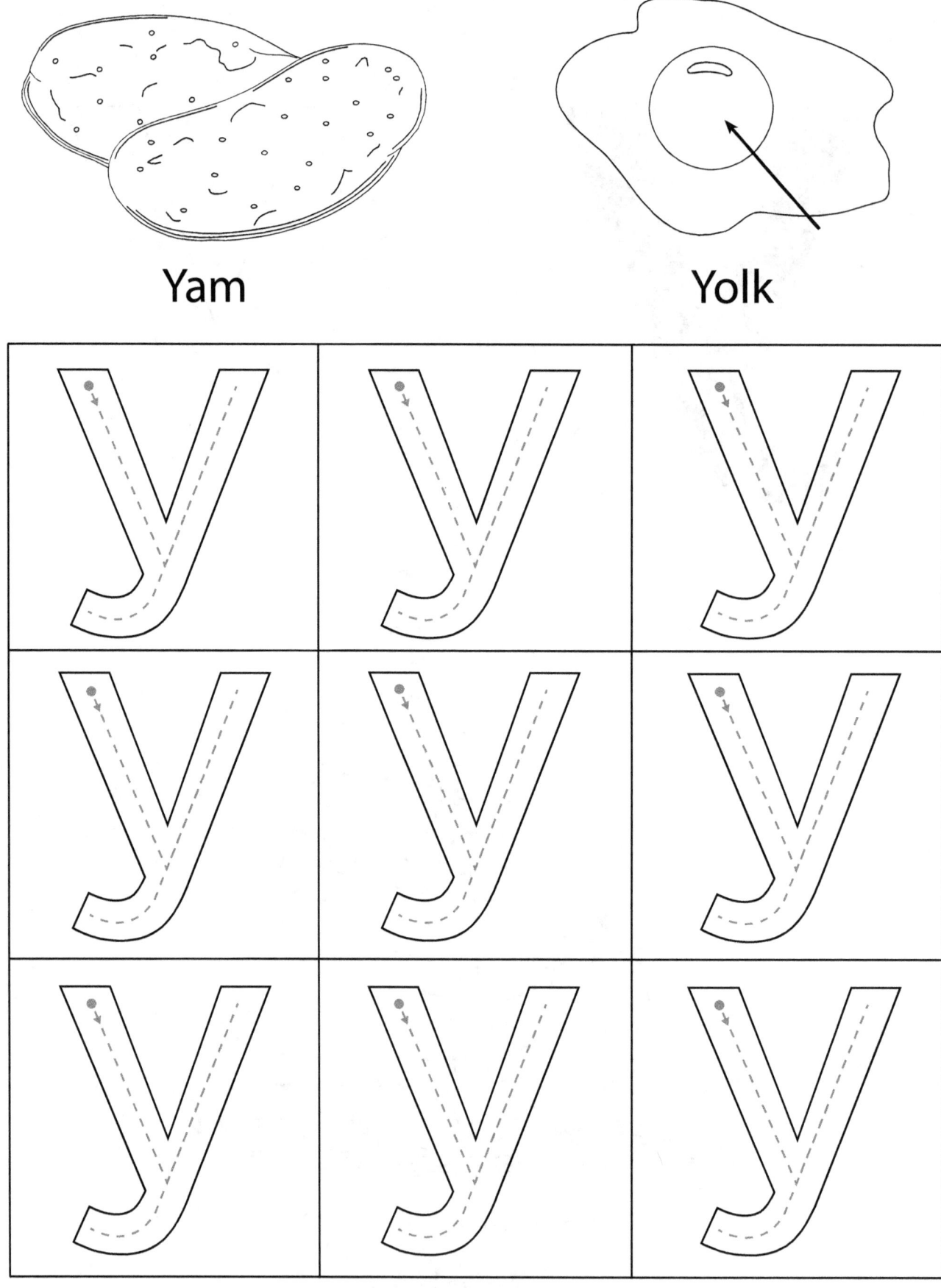

Yam   Yolk

trace and color

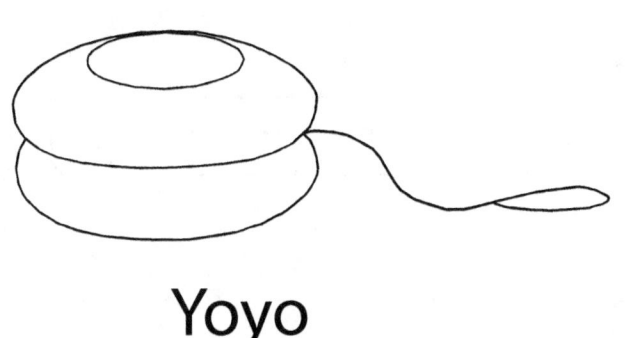
Yoyo

Yak

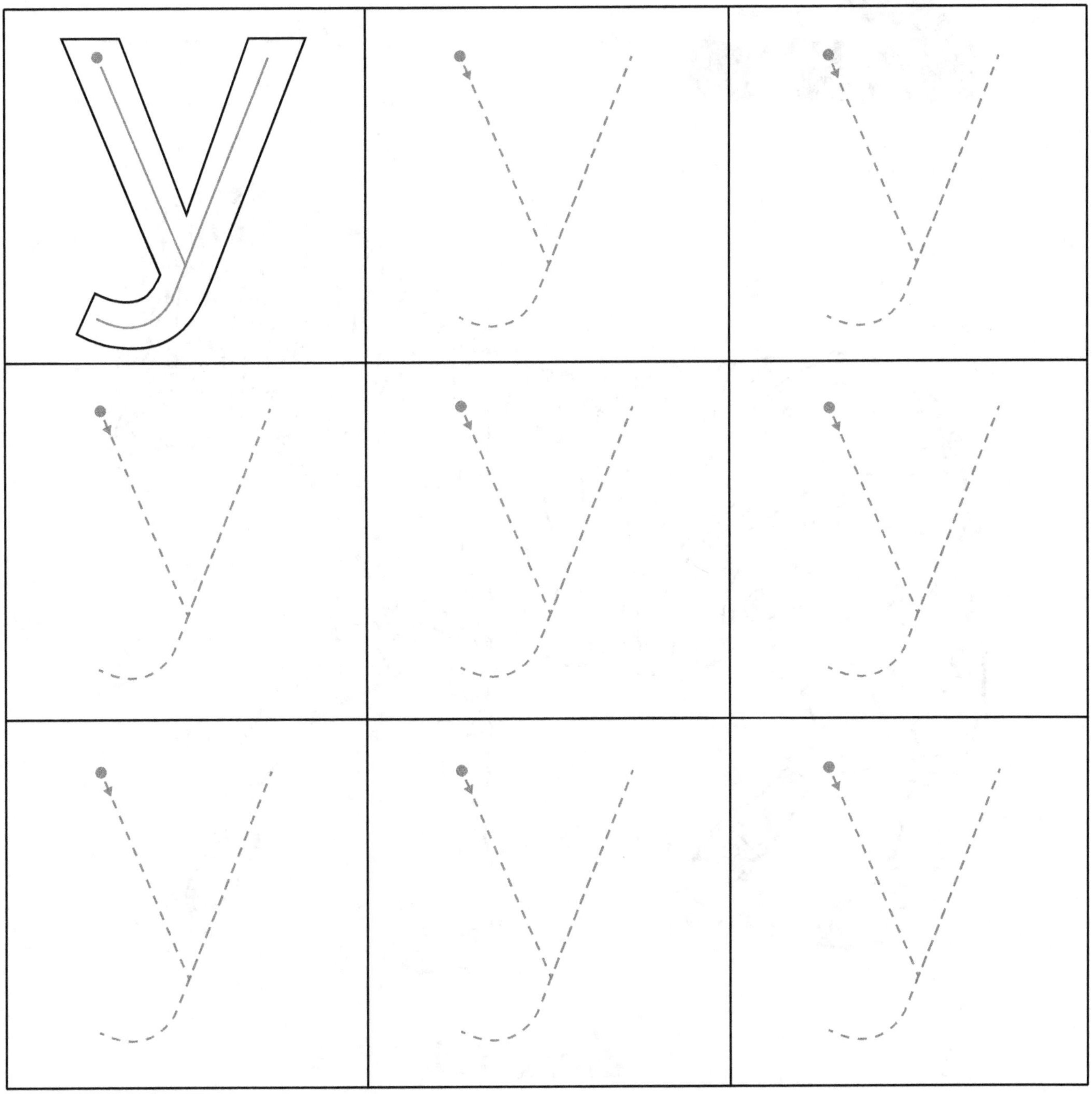

trace and color

Z Z

Zebra

trace and color

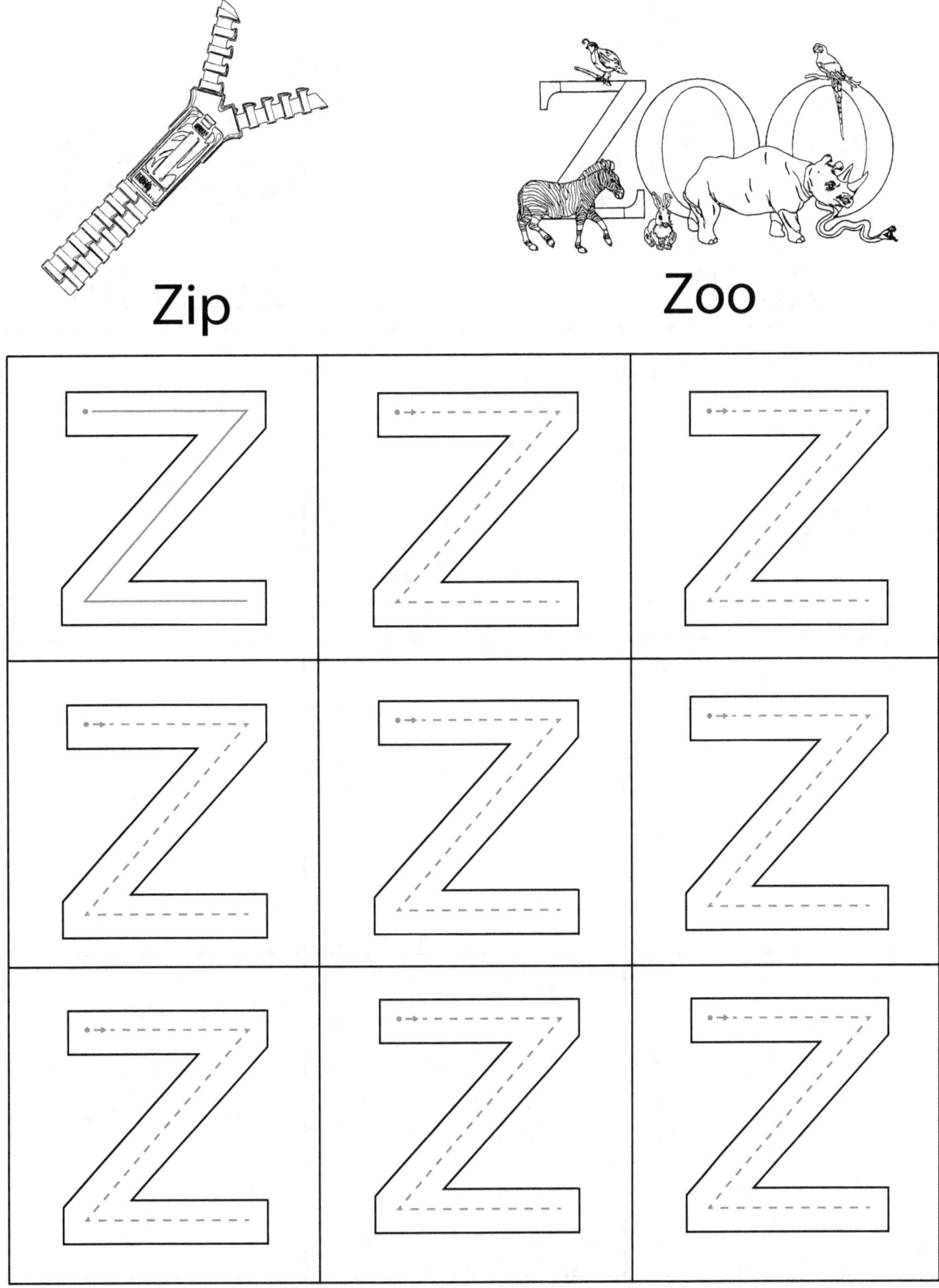

Zip   Zoo

trace and color

Zorilla

Zucchini

match the same sounds

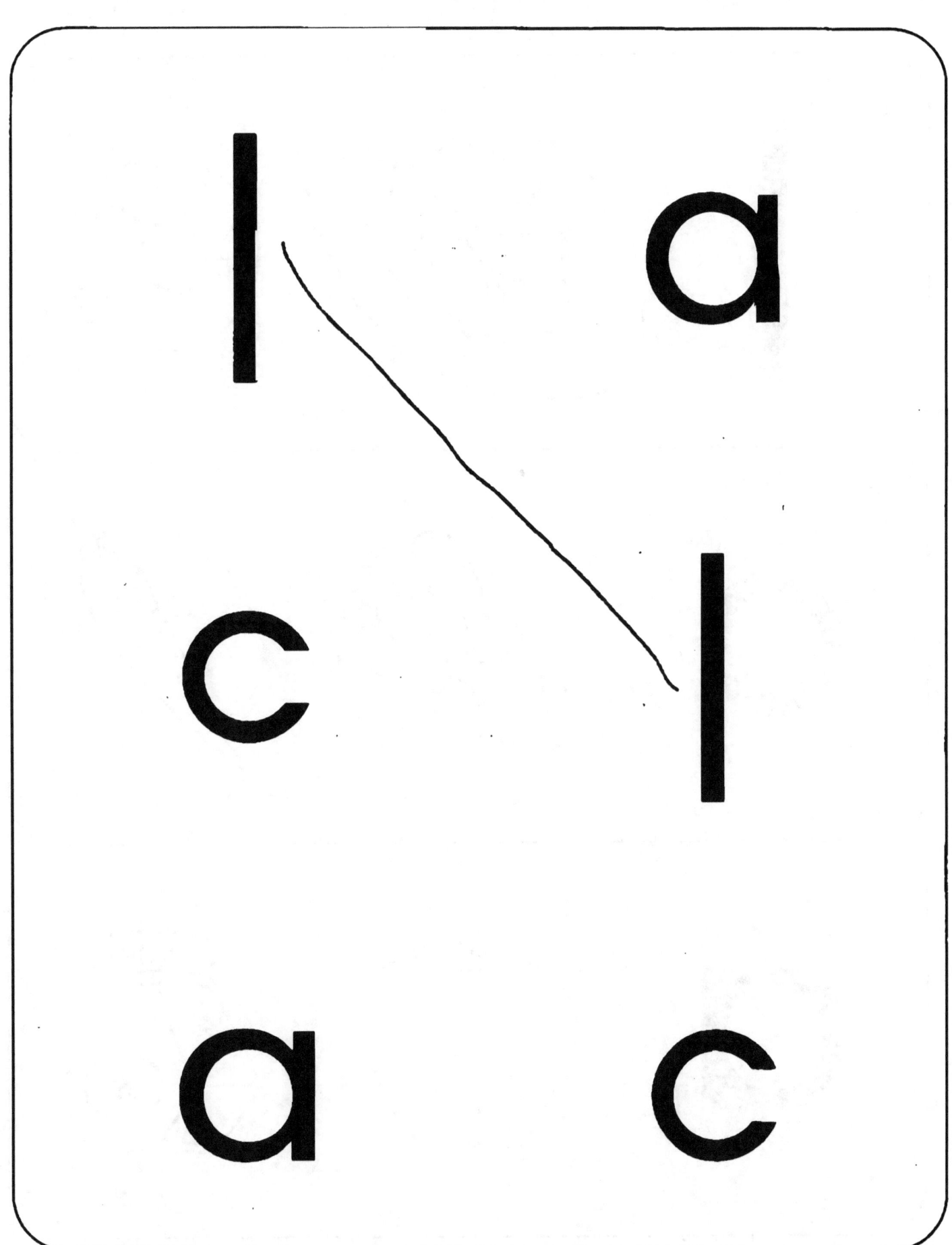

circle the correct picture

match the pictures with correct beginning sounds

write and say the sounds

r	n	a	d
.	.	.	.
.	.	.	.
.	.	.	.
.	.	.	.
.	.	.	.

write and say the sounds

match the pictures with correct beginning sounds

circle the correct beginning sound

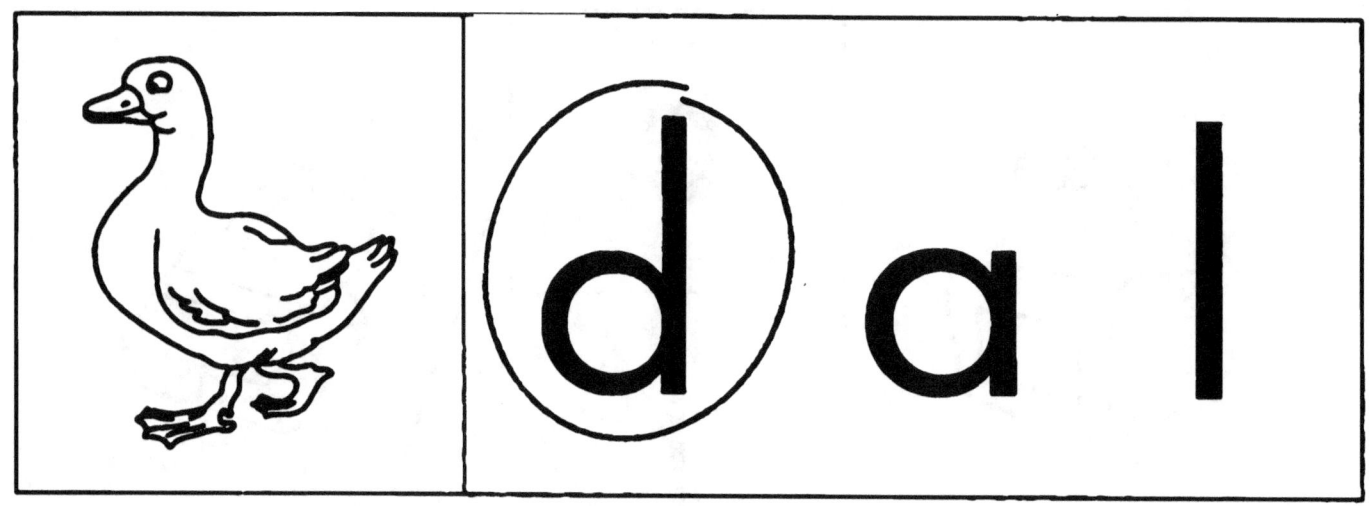

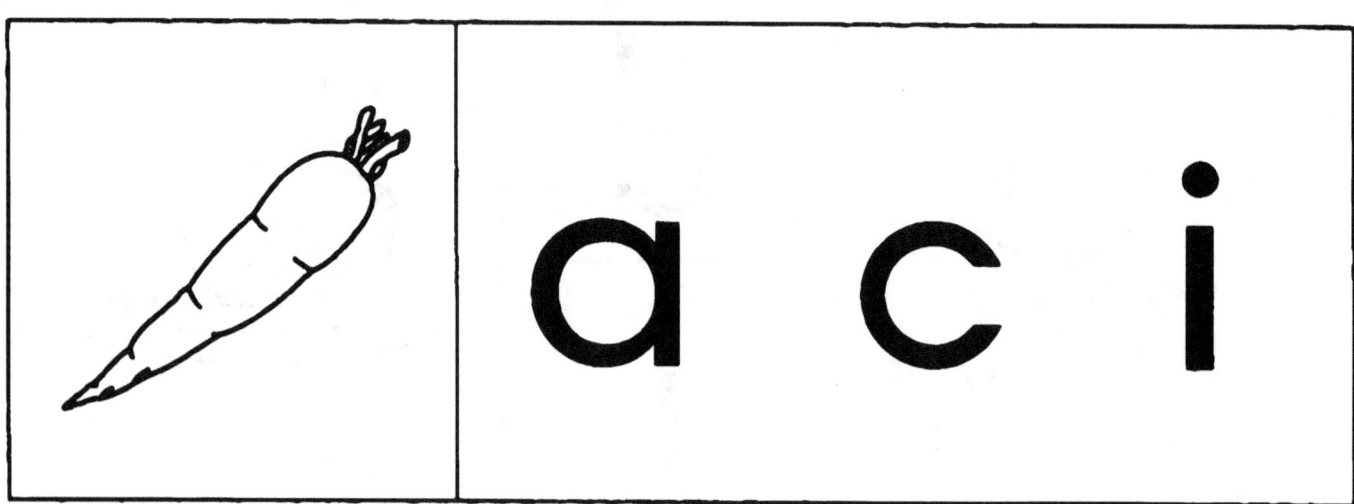

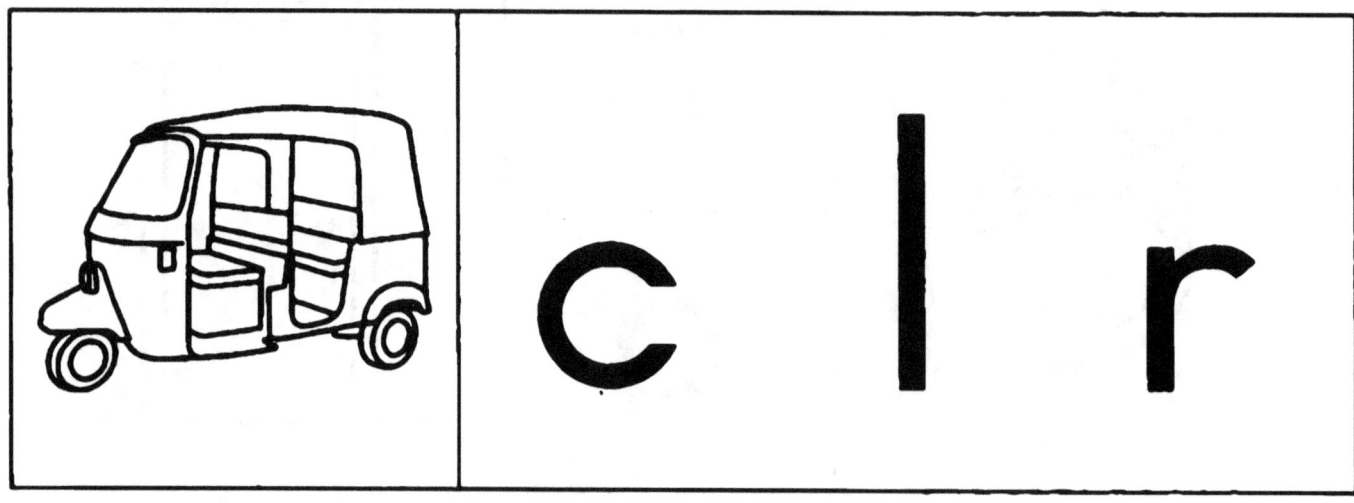

circle the correct picture

www.ingramcontent.com/pod-product-compliance
Lightning Source LLC
LaVergne TN
LVHW060210080526
838202LV00052B/4239